the BURNING BOOK

BCC PRESS

BY COMMON CONSENT PRESS is a non-profit publisher dedicated to producing affordable, high-quality books that help define and shape the Latter-day Saint experience. BCC Press publishes books that address all aspects of Mormon life. Our mission includes finding manuscripts that will contribute to the lives of thoughtful Latter-day Saints, mentoring authors and nurturing projects to completion, and distributing important books to the Mormon audience at the lowest possible cost.

JASON OLSON + JAMES GOLDBERG

the BURNING BOOK

A JEWISH-MORMON MEMOIR

For information contact
By Common Consent Press
4900 Penrose Dr.
Newburgh, IN 47630

Cover design: D Christian Harrison
Book design: Andrew Heiss

www.bccpress.org
ISBN-13: 978-1-948218-57-3

This book does not represent the views or policies of the U.S. Department of Defense. Views and information are the authors' alone.

10 9 8 7 6 5 4 3 2 1

To Sara, my forever and a day
—Jason

CONTENTS

◇

PROLOGUE

◇

When I came into this world, I was named twice.

On American government documents my parents filled out at the hospital, I was Jason Olson. My mother, who is Jewish, chose the name Jason as a wish: it means "healer" in Greek, and she hoped I'd bring more healing than hurt into the world. Olson comes from my father's Lutheran family. No one has any idea anymore which son of an Ole first got the name, but it's been handed down to us.

Eight days later, when I was circumcised, I was given a Hebrew name: Yehoshua ben Yona. Yehoshua, the root name of the English name Joshua, sounds a little like Jason, though it refers not to one who heals but to one who delivers. Ben means "son of" (so many cultures recognize how much your identity comes from your parents). Yona is my mother's Hebrew name.

It was important to my dad that we celebrate Christmas and Easter, but my parents had agreed I would be raised Jewish. With that Hebrew name, my mother gave me more than a few syllables to use at our temple. She gave me a world that had been handed down from mother to child for generations. She invited me to carry a covenant my ancestors made at Mount

Sinai millennia ago, a covenant that bound God to a people and bound a people to God.

My maternal ancestors clung to that covenant over thousands of years and through bitter persecution. They carried it from their ancient homes in Israel into exile in Babylon and back. They carried it into the Diaspora after the Romans destroyed Jerusalem and scattered much of our people far from their promised land. In European Jewish settlements, or *shtetls*, like my great-great grandparents' village of Bogopol in what is now Ukraine, they endured discrimination and violence by Christian neighbors and rulers.

Why did my ancestors stay faithful to their tradition under generations of pressure? Probably because, like me, they loved what Judaism gave them.

To me, being a Jew meant hearing the beat of a divine drummer. The law, so often viewed with derision by Christians, brought a divine calibration to our people. It brought a sense of sacred order syncing our calendar and daily life with God's heartbeat. Growing up, that rhythm meant the world to me. I cherished the simple taste of Passover matzah against the sharpness of bitter herbs. I loved the Chanukah candles and the sense of connection with other Jews around the world and across time as we set the lights burning against the darkness of night. I longed for the annual fast on Yom Kippur, the holiest day of the year, when the windows of heaven open in grace and the repentant person's sins against God are forgiven.

To me, being a Jew was about receiving that divinely revealed way of life that brings joy. It was about receiving it from your ancestors and passing it to your children. It was about centering your life on the Torah.

But to me, and to those who came before me, being a Jew also means to be in conflict—with the past, with the dominant culture, with oneself, even with God. After all, the name Israel can mean "those who wrestle with God," a continual spiritual grappling with divinity.

In my life, that wrestle with God led me all the way into another faith. When I was eighteen years old, I became a member of the Church of Jesus Christ of Latter-day Saints. At the time, I not only witnessed my acceptance of new religious beliefs—I also stepped into another line of legacy, another history. I cast in my lot with the Mormon people.

But none of that took away my roots, or the Hebrew name my mother gave me.

Like Jacob, who left limping after his night with the angel, I have stumbled forward as I've tried to work out what it means to be true to myself, my ancestors, and my God. My purpose in this book is not to convert anyone—to call the reader down one religious path or another—but to reflect on the layers of my own identity. Not many Jewish kids grow up to go on Mormon missions. Not many Mormon returned missionaries go searching for their Jewish souls in the land of Israel or in a Jewish Studies PhD program at Brandeis.

Working with my friend James Goldberg, a writer drawn to multicultural stories, I've tried to trace the threads of my life across two faiths and two countries. It's hard not to let the expectations people have for what a conversion story ought to look like shape the way you tell it, but I've done my best to be true to the complexity I lived: the loss and gain, the pain and blessing.

Some aspects of the religious world I come from may be unfamiliar to readers. I've included a glossary of Jewish terms at the end of the book to help readers navigate that side of my story, plus a Q&A to address some of the questions my life story raises. I should note that virtually every reader will find places to disagree with my commitments religiously, socially, or politically—and I wouldn't have it any other way. But I hope you can see the humanity in my story and relate, in your own particular way, to my winding journey.

—Jason Olson, June 2021

PART ONE

THE COVENANT PATH

CHAPTER ONE

SON OF THE COMMANDMENTS

◇

I became a bar mitzvah, a son of the commandments, on June 27, 1998.

To get ready for that day, I practiced for months. During a bar mitzvah, you stand before the congregation and chant a passage from the Torah scroll. As a child, I'd learned the sounds Hebrew consonants make, but there's a lot more to reading a Torah scroll than that. Our cantor had made a cassette tape for me so I could learn the melody that traditionally went with the passage, and I'd listen to her voice over and over again to get it just right. I was also meeting regularly with one of the rabbis at our Reform synagogue to work on my d'var Torah, a brief talk giving my own commentary. She'd talk with me about the passage, about what it got me thinking about, about how to share my thoughts in a worship setting. Even though I was only thirteen, it was important to me to give people a meaningful experience. Some kids focus most of their attention on the party their families throw afterward, but for me this wasn't just a celebration: it was a spiritual event.

My Torah portion was Parashat Korach. It begins in Numbers 16, when the children of Israel are wandering in the wilderness. At the beginning, a man named Korach leads a rebellion against Moses' authority. Korach's allies accuse Moses of setting himself above them. They say he's led them out to the wilderness to die. It's a larger pattern: even though they've been miraculously delivered from slavery in Egypt, there are always people who get tired of following Moses' vision. Once that happens, it's easy to see him not as a prophet, but as an oppressor. Moses complains to God: he says he never took so much as a donkey from any of them. He asks God to judge between him and the rebels—and the next day, the earth opens up to swallow Korach and his faction.

Reviewing it over and over again, I imagined myself there. Wondered whether I would have been swayed at all. The stories of Moses lit a fire in me like a burning bush. They drew me in and offered me a genuine awe. I didn't want to be someone who threw that away: I wanted to believe I'd be willing to follow him, that I'd be faithful in the journey through whatever wilderness a prophet led me through.

When the day of my bar mitzvah approached, my mom's parents—Grandma Gilda and Papa Al—came down from Chicago to our home in Scottsdale, Arizona to be there. They usually came around Chanukah, bringing gifts that had changed from Teenage Mutant Ninja Turtle toys when I was little to Nintendo 64 games as I got older. This time they brought something different: as my bar mitzvah service began, Grandma Gilda stepped up to clothe me in a tallit, a prayer shawl, to prepare me to take my place in the community and before God. While my father watched from the congregation, Grandma Gilda, Papa Al, and my mother came with me onto the bimah, the raised platform at the front of the synagogue, while I said the blessings to open the ark where the Torah scroll is kept. Rabbi Tzur handed the scroll to them and they passed it along to me. Like a trust. It meant a lot to take the scroll from Papa Al, who had served in the US Army during World War Two fighting Nazism, from Grandma Gilda, from my mother, and carry it around the congregation before coming back to chant my Torah portion and give my sermon.

All the preparation paid off. I felt good about what I was able to share. I felt good about being formally accepted as a grown member of the Jewish community, even if I was only thirteen years old. After my sermon was finished, I remember Rabbi Tzur laying her hands on my head in blessing. And I remember feeling, for just a moment, this distinct closeness to God. Like God was there, too, welcoming me.

I was glad to feel God's presence. I was proud to be Jewish. I wouldn't have wanted it any other way.

◇ ▢ ◇

From a historical perspective, Arizona in the 1990s was a pretty easy place to grow up as a Jew. Our local community was just starting to come of age. We lived in neighborhoods that were more religiously mixed than my grandparents had known in Chicago, but there was still a critical mass of Jews around. Individuals and families could choose to worship with a congregation in the Reform movement, in the Conservative movement, or even study at the Phoenix community kollel with rabbis who were Modern Orthodox. Around the time of my bar mitzvah, plans were also being made to build a new, shared Jewish Community Center in Scottsdale with classrooms and a gym to replace the little offices in downtown Phoenix that had served the smaller Jewish community for so long. While a lot of people's grandparents or great-grandparents had been immigrants from countries where they were treated like second-class citizens, our parents were mostly transplants from the Midwest or California, people who had always known religious freedom.

Even in my generation, though, religious freedom didn't always mean we were treated with tolerance and respect. I remember, when I was about twelve, hanging out with a Christian friend and his cousin. Apparently, their evangelical church had preached vividly about what happens to people who don't accept Christ. At one point, when no one else was around, my friend's cousin cornered me in the garage and confronted me about what he saw as my religious shortcomings. "Jason, I need you to confess Jesus as your Lord and Savior with your mouth, or you will be damned," he told me, standing too close. I was just a kid. I didn't get the Protestant theology of salvation by faith alone, didn't understand why it was so important to him that I say a certain phrase or how that was supposed to save me. I doubt he grasped all the theology, either. He just knew that I was a Jew and Jews had rejected Jesus and that we needed to be brought into line or we would go to hell. I just knew this felt really weird and uncomfortable.

Another time, some of us were playing tackle football at our neighborhood park. No pads, no helmets. Just a brutal kind of fun in the Arizona desert heat. The grass barely grew in the sandy field. We still liked to run and laugh and mess around. On this particular day, not long before my bar mitzvah, some other kids from the school who didn't like us much came by the park on their bikes.

At my school, it wasn't hard to figure out who was Jewish because we took the Jewish holidays off. These boys knew who we were. Maybe they thought that having our own holidays made us weird? Or maybe they just thought it would make them feel tough to pick on somebody else. Anyway, they got off their bikes and started making fun of us and shoving us around. As we got into a yelling match, one of them shouted, "You Jews should go back to the gas chambers!"

It was the first time I got into a fistfight.

That was America. We weren't told we had to live in a certain part of town or only in a certain part of the country, like a lot of European Jews had. In school, students read books about what Jews had gone through in the Holocaust. They were taught we should never let something like that happen again. And still, there were the moments when it felt like people wanted us wiped out: physically, culturally, or spiritually.

Years later, I heard a Jewish scholar describe my growing up years as being haunted by an idea called Jewish survivalism. The idea was that if young Jews broke the chain of identity, Hitler could still get what he wanted. The Nazis could still win. You can see why people would feel that way in a world where their kids' peers were still making offhand comments about the gas chambers, where friends would push you to say Jesus was your savior as the only way to avoid eternal damnation. You can also see why they would say that in a place where Jews were so broadly accepted otherwise, it was easier to marry Christians. Like my mom did. They worried that, one way or another, the Jewish community wouldn't be able to hold on to my friends, and that it might be especially doomed to lose a lot of kids with one Christian parent. Like me.

◇ ▢ ◇

At the age of fourteen, early in the fall of my freshman year of high school, the Hebrew High youth program at my Reform synagogue invited a special guest speaker late one Wednesday night. He sheepishly entered our high-walled, reverent sanctuary in a "Jews for Jesus" T-shirt and introduced himself as a missionary named Mitch.

Something seemed very wrong. We worried Christian missionaries in general might turn out to be just a few steps of civility away from the Spanish inquisition, where thousands of Jews had to choose between forced conversion or death, but felt most upset by groups like Jews for Jesus. These groups, which used a claim of Jewish identity in their attempts to Christianize Jews, seemed to us fundamentally dishonest: like wolves in sheep's clothing. Offering religious assimilation wrapped in the trappings of Jewish identity.

Mitch didn't seem to notice our discomfort. He simply announced, "Your rabbis have invited me tonight to share my perspective on why you should accept Jesus, our Jewish Messiah, today."

As he spoke, there was an uproar through the sanctuary. Youth all around me were interrupting Mitch to call out to the rabbis, "What are you thinking!? Why'd you invite this 'missionary' into our holy place?"

The rabbis told us to be patient. "We want you to hear both sides of this," they said. "This is important. After Mitch, we'll have another speaker present our traditional Jewish point of view on Christianity. For now, let's respectfully listen to Mitch and what he has to say."

At least where I was sitting (front row, far left side), my friends weren't impressed with the rabbis' dispassionate calm. This wasn't just about hearing another perspective. This was offensive. "Why do we need to listen to this Mitch guy at all?" they asked me. "Jason, let's grab him and 'escort' him out."

I could be as quick as anyone to defend Judaism. My friends knew I wouldn't back down if I felt like my identity was under attack. But I trusted our rabbis. "I don't know, guys," I said. "Let's just let Mitch say his piece and we can debate about it afterwards."

As the room calmed down, Mitch proceeded, "I know you've all been taught that Jesus died before the Messianic Age and so there is no way he can be our Messiah. Well, I'm here to tell you that his death is what saves you from your sins! Jesus took upon himself all our sins on the cross. He is the suffering servant promised to us in Isaiah 53."

Despite having a Christian father, my understanding of the faith didn't go much beyond baby Jesus being related to the Christmas tree. I didn't know much about Christian scripture. The reference to Isaiah surprised me. At this point, I was thinking, "Wait . . . Jesus' death on the cross was prophesied in the Tanakh, in our Hebrew Bible?"

Mitch continued, "And the Holy Spirit has witnessed to me that three of you have accepted Jesus into your heart this day."

That caught me off guard, too. I'd just been thinking about the prophecy in Isaiah: did that make me one of the three? Had I accepted Jesus into my heart without realizing it? I was confused. I felt a little guilty, knowing this was surely not what the rabbis wanted from Mitch's visit.

It wasn't what I wanted, either. I could still remember how excited I'd been to learn the Hebrew words and melody for the passage I'd read at my bar mitzvah. On that day, I had committed my life to Judaism. So what did it mean if it was the Holy Spirit witnessing to me that Jesus was the Messiah?

My confusion was deep and profound. I didn't want to be a rebel like Korach in the Torah. Perhaps I simply felt torn between my loyalty to my mother and Judaism, and to the Christian culture and faith of my father. If the scriptures supported both, what was I supposed to do? Who was right; or were they all wrong together?

At that alarming moment, Mitch left the sanctuary. My friends watched him all the way down the pews, until he exited the doors and was out of our hair. The commotion continued, though, with students muttering about the rabbis' obvious lapse in judgment.

"I'm going to tell my parents!" I remember one friend saying. "Do you really think we'll keep attending this synagogue after this?" Others just asked the rabbis what on earth they *had* been thinking.

"Just hang on now," the rabbis said. "We promised you that you would hear our traditional Jewish side. Please wait a few moments, patiently. Our second speaker will be here soon."

While we waited for the second speaker, they asked us, "So, what did you think about Mitch and his presentation of Christianity?"

"This is a *Jewish* synagogue," someone said. "This is insane."

As students started to get worked up again, the rabbis

assured us everything was under control.

"Please, just wait for our next speaker. This will all make sense then," they said.

Calming ourselves down, but still with anxiety and excitement, we watched the second speaker arrive. It was Mitch again! Only now the "Jews for Jesus" T-shirt was gone and he was wearing a kippah and tallit. He looked like an Orthodox rabbi.

Okay, now we might really need to escort him out of our sanctuary. He said his piece, now it's time for him to go! I thought.

Mitch addressed us again., "I'm sorry for confusing you about who I really am," he said. "My name is Rabbi Tovia Singer. I'm an Orthodox Rabbi and the founder of Outreach Judaism, a ministry designed to lead Jews back to Judaism. Your rabbis invited me here to show you a hands-on example of how 'Jews for Jesus' missionaries will try to deceptively convert you to Christianity. I'm here to train you with the knowledge necessary to defend your Judaism from their evangelism."

I was floored. I felt disoriented, and a little betrayed that our rabbis had fooled us on purpose.

"Christian Jews are not real Jews. They are Christians," Rabbi Singer taught. It was in our interest, he said, to prepare ourselves against their methods.

He started by debunking the Christian understanding of Isaiah 53. He taught us that, in the Hebrew original, the suffering servant is the entire Jewish people, not the Messiah as an individual.

Rabbi Singer also argued Jesus did not fulfill a single prophecy of the Messiah in the Hebrew Bible. His case was convincing. We all knew the song "David, Melech Yisrael"—David, King of Israel. For us, the hope of a Messiah who would restore Israel and rule over a golden age was not a distant historical memory. The image of a Messianic age was still woven into our faith. It was easy enough, knowing Jesus had died without inaugurating an age of justice and redemption, to believe Rabbi Singer's claim that Jesus could not have been the Messiah. I took his word for it that other Christian claims didn't add up.

As I listened to Rabbi Singer speak with confidence and authority, I felt foolish. Why had I been so ready to identify myself as one of the three people "Mitch," a fake missionary, had said accepted Jesus in their hearts? A part of me wondered whether, having a Christian father, I was inherently more susceptible to being misled.

The challenge felt so real. Up to this point in my life, I had never been asked to make such a stark choice in terms of my beliefs about Jesus. I was only asked to express doubt or misgivings about Jesus' Messiahship, never to outright reject him. Before this experience, I thought it was cool that I had a Jewish mother and a Christian father. The Reform rabbis, who placed a high value on tolerance, did not teach me to view Christians generally as a threat. My view was that we Jews were to live in harmony with the Christians. We were not to try to dismantle their faith.

"Christianity is a beautiful religion," our head rabbi, Rabbi Berk, had once said in Hebrew school. "And we honor our Christian neighbors in their faith. But as Jews, Christianity is not for us." Listening to that lesson, it had felt simple enough to support my Christian father so long as I didn't embrace his private beliefs. They could remain something I knew about that we just happened not to talk about.

Rabbi Singer, though, made it clear that we may well need to counter missionaries' arguments to maintain our loyalty as Jews. Rabbi Singer's words stirred a deep Jewish pride in me. I liked his Orthodox seriousness and clarity. I felt addressed by his urgency. If Christians were so ready to undermine our faith, I thought, I needed to be more prepared. Even at the expense of convenient tolerance.

Was I now to become a modern Abraham, destroying the Christian idols of my pagan father? That was the zeal I was feeling from Rabbi Singer.

As a fourteen-year-old boy, with a simple understanding

of religion and culture, I suddenly felt like I needed to choose between the Judaism I'd inherited from my mother and my father's Christian traditions. That choice felt particularly significant because I had already wondered if I wanted to stick with the norms of Reform Judaism forever or eventually embrace the rigors of a Modern Orthodox life. After my meaningful bar mitzvah, I was just hungry for more. Reform Judaism did well at passing on Jewish identity, but didn't seem as interested to me in religious law and overt spirituality. It was clear, though, that Orthodox Jews would be uncomfortable with me embracing some of the lifestyle of my Christian father, like celebrating Christmas and Easter with him. Coming from a mixed household, I might be asked to make some changes to live an Orthodox life. So I needed to know what to do.

My soul was on fire. The status quo I had lived with all my life was breaking down. I could not just be the interesting mixed kid who got presents for Hanukkah and Christmas. Rabbi Singer challenged me. He confused me. My house was divided—but I was determined not to let my heart be.

◇ ▢ ◇

What was someone like me to do? After heading back home that night, Rabbi Singer's challenge to arm myself with Jewish knowledge as a defense against missionaries still echoed through my mind. To accomplish that, I decided to invest more effort in my own study of the Bible. I needed to understand what it really said about the Messiah.

While the general hope for a Messiah had been part of my religious upbringing, Reform Judaism was not terribly interested in details. Most of my Reform rabbis did not even believe the Messiah was going to be a person. They focused more on the concept of a Messianic Age, a representation of a healed world. For me, those general hopes and a focus on good behavior in the current climate were compelling, but not quite enough. I found Rabbi Singer's conviction of a coming personal Messiah much more moving.

So, I started with Rabbi Singer's Outreach Judaism website. To complement the modern feel of my reading on the computer, I pulled out the beautiful, hardbound *ArtScroll* Hebrew-English Tanakh I had received as a gift for my bar mitzvah. I liked the weight of the book. I liked the smell of its pages. For me as a teenager, the scent of study was already inviting. I felt like I was getting into something deep and real. I intuitively trusted the feel of the heavy volume of scripture in my hands.

Which was good, because I intended to study all the prophecies of the Messiah found anywhere in it.

On his website, Rabbi Singer presented the major Biblical proof-texts Christians use as evidence that Jesus was the Messiah. I studied these texts carefully and then supplemented them with what his website presented as a proper, correct Jewish interpretation. At the time, Rabbi Singer convinced me that Judaism was objectively correct in its rejection of Jesus as Messiah. As I studied the Hebrew prophecies of the Messiah, it was clear that although Jesus attempted to fulfill them, he ultimately failed to fulfill all of them during his lifetime. I could look around me and see that the world was not redeemed, the dead not risen.

I felt like I was on to something. Rabbi Singer was the first rabbi I'd encountered who presented a direct and serious challenge to Christian teachings. If I was to become an Orthodox Jew, like him, I felt I needed to master the ideas behind his rejection of Christianity.

After the Rabbi Singer event, I decided to personally ask Rabbi Berk, "Why don't we accept Jesus as the Messiah?"

He was a lot more cautious, more subjective. "Well, in my rabbinical studies at Hebrew Union College, we studied the New Testament," he told me. "There are a lot of errors in it and mistranslations of the Tanakh. The New Testament is just unreliable for us as Jews."

That was unsatisfying to me. I was still confused. I hadn't been through theological school. I didn't know enough Hebrew and Greek to make my own assessments. Unsatisfied, I increasingly turned to Rabbi Singer's detailed website, the only major Jewish counter-missionary website at the time. I was voracious. Even though it's frowned upon in Jewish communities to mark up scripture, I underlined every prophecy about the Messiah I could find in that *Artscroll* Tanakh. I didn't want to lose track of any of it.

I was determined to become the greatest counter-missionary Jew. (Clearly my confidence in Rabbi Singer's approach to Judaism was as strong as my ego.) I figured I had preparation. Now, I only needed practice. With real Christians: not just characters like "Mitch."

◇ ◻ ◇

As it happened, I knew some Christians I could try out my new abilities on. In my 7th grade math class, I'd met Shea Owens. He was kind of a prankster, which had led to spending our first and only detention together, but I knew he had a strong core of religious conviction.

One time, we'd been hanging out at a friend's house where there were *Playboy* magazines. Almost everyone started ogling the pictures in them, but Shea didn't. Even when one kid opened up the centerfold and put it right in front of Shea, he turned his head aside and said, "I don't want to look at that. Please put it away or I'm going home." I didn't want him excluded because of a moral conviction, so I said, "Yeah, we shouldn't look at that stuff with Shea here. He's a Mormon, y'know."

I wasn't immune to peer pressure, so I admired Shea for resisting it. Like most middle school kids, I wanted to fit in and have everybody like me. I remember the most popular kid in school, Mark, giving me my shot. "Jason, you're cool," he said.

What a compliment! "Why don't you come sit with me and my friends during lunch?" *What an invitation!*

To me, that felt like I'd just scored a ticket to a future of getting invited to all the best parties, catching the eye of all the cutest girls. I sat with Mark and his friends at lunch for a couple of days. The other boys were welcoming. We played Pop Warner football together, and it didn't hurt that I was good. We talked about football. We talked about girls. And then Mark invited me to come over after school and hang out because he'd scored some weed.

My heart sank. That wasn't the path I wanted. I didn't make any excuses: I just told Mark no. He was kind of hurt. Even the cool kid wants to feel cool. Even Mark wanted to feel liked, to feel like people were excited by what he could offer. I don't think anyone had ever turned him down before. After I did, I stopped sitting with his friend group at lunch.

I went back to sitting with Shea after that. I didn't need to say anything about my experience, though he must have noticed something because he started trying to sell me on joining choir. He told me it was good, clean fun. And choir had plenty of girls. Maybe the choir kids were a little dorky, but I decided to give it a shot. My friendship with Shea blossomed after that.

I could be myself around him, and he could be himself around me. That made it easier not to care about being cool. We invented our own fun. He appreciated my commitment to Judaism and I liked having a Mormon friend who I trusted to keep me away from drugs.

Shea's friend Dave Thaxton was the same way. Mormon kids weren't like other Christians. In a school full of Catholics and Protestants, they knew what it meant to be a religious minority. They also didn't seem to have the "sin all you want; Jesus will forgive you" attitude I perceived in Christianity generally. Shea and Dave believed that God cared about moral order. That mattered to me.

Like other Christians, of course, Shea and Dave believed Jesus was the Messiah. And they were serious about it: both planned to serve as missionaries someday.

And as future missionaries, they were the perfect practice for me to apply Rabbi Singer's teachings. I had read highlighted prophecy after prophecy, had read through commentary I found convincing. Like most people, I figured other people would see things the way I did if I just talked them through the steps right. I believed I could convince my high school Latter-day Saint friends that they were wrong about Jesus being the promised Messiah.

If you ask a Mormon to talk religion, they're already primed to say yes. And if you don't start in by announcing they've been brainwashed into an evil cult, they're game for pretty much anything else. We met for weeks during lunch, debating the points of Judaism and Christianity. I wanted to test out Rabbi Singer's ideas on them. I wanted to strengthen myself by seeking out opposition. I believed opposition would lead to growth. If I could defend myself against these future missionaries as a freshman, I would surely have the strength to protect myself from more sophisticated missionaries later. And I assumed that my deep dive into Tovia Singer's website and the passages I'd highlighted made me by far the most religiously experienced.

I had no idea my Latter-day Saint friends were studying the Old Testament in their early morning seminary class that year.

CHAPTER TWO

DISCUSSION AND DEBATE

◇

Sitting at a brown metal table in the corner of the high school cafeteria, I had started watching Shea Owens and Dave Thaxton discuss religion over lunch with a Catholic friend of ours, Matt Lorimer. Shea and Dave sat on one side of the table, and Matt and I on the other. At first, they talked about the differences between Catholicism and Mormonism. But this wasn't going to be a Christians-only conversation. When I sensed an opportunity, I had begun to share my skepticism about the Biblical case that Jesus was the Messiah.

I talked them through the different things the Messiah was supposed to do, and they seemed genuinely interested. I noted how Jesus failed to measure up, and they seemed more skeptical. Then I opted for bluntness instead of my rabbis' gentle tolerance. "You have it all wrong to base your entire religion on Jesus," I said simply.

Dave wasn't upset, but he wasn't convinced either. He explained how he and Shea were getting up before dawn each day to go study the scriptures with other Latter-day Saint youth.

They felt connected to the prophets, felt like they needed to understand their message. And yes, they thought that Messianic prophecies were an important part of what the prophets had to say. When I explained how Jesus had failed to fulfill those prophecies, Dave was totally unfazed. That didn't bother him, he explained, because he believed that many prophecies would be fulfilled at Jesus' Second Coming. "You're right that Jesus has not fulfilled all those prophecies yet," he said. "But I have faith that he will." Echoing language from Isaiah, he said he believed in a Messiah who was both lamb and lion.

I was impressed by Dave's easy confidence. Though he clearly cared about what the Hebrew Bible—his Old Testament—said, he didn't seem worried about proving me wrong. He was content just to share his convictions, plus answer any follow-up questions I had.

This was the first time any Christians had ever explained the Second Coming to me, so I had a lot of questions. As we kept talking, it became clear that my Mormon friends believed in a lot of the same expectations about the Messiah that I'd learned from Rabbi Singer. They didn't think of Jesus only as a universal Savior. They didn't think redemption was only a matter of confessing his name. Somehow, they'd kept a little more of what I understood to be the original context. It was clear they were concerned about God's covenant with the House of Israel. They believed in the ultimate redemption of the Jewish people, just like I did.

And they had thought about a lot of things I hadn't expected Christians to talk about. It came up, for example, that they had a deep respect for the Temple in Biblical Jerusalem and believed that Jesus would have it rebuilt when he returned.

Two thousand years after it was destroyed by the Romans, the Temple's presence still echoes through Judaism. Part of our sacred calendar is a day to mourn its destruction. References to the Temple come up in the traditions for most Jewish holidays, from the egg on the seder tray at Passover to the

Chanukah lights, which commemorate a miracle during the cleansing and sanctification of the Temple after it was defiled by intolerant Greek rulers.

"You know, Jason," Dave told me, "we really love temples in our Church too. We worship in them, just like the ancient Jews did."

I didn't know how similar their worship might really be, but it surprised me that they worshipped in temples at all. I asked if that was a common belief, but as far as Dave knew, Latter-day Saints were the only Christians who emphasized temple worship.

We kept eating lunch together every day and discussing new topics. It wasn't always religion: we'd laugh, joke, talk about crushes. We always circled back to questions of belief, though. I kept stretching my Latter-day Saint friends, questioning them incessantly. But their patience never seemed to run out. They didn't mind listening to me, being challenged by me. They didn't get defensive. They showed respect for, and interest in, my beliefs. But they also had real answers about theirs.

As our discussions became more personal, the cafeteria stopped feeling like enough. It was always loud and sometimes rowdy. We needed a better place. A more reverent place. Dave and I decided to stay after school and talk more in the library. We sat in a private corner where we could speak freely, if only in librarian-approved whispers.

During one of those library sessions, Dave finally built up the courage to offer me a Book of Mormon he and Shea had gotten for me. "Jason," he said, "it's been fun discussing religion with you these past months. We thought you might benefit from reading the Book of Mormon. It's our sacred book of scripture and it's my honor to give you one." He and Shea had handwritten their testimonies, short statements of conviction, in it.

I felt strange. On the one hand, I was curious about their

religion. Their approach seemed so flexible and faithful. I had grown especially curious about what made the Latter-day Saints different from other Christians. All I could remember being taught at Hebrew High was that the Book of Mormon was about gold plates and Native Americans, but there was clearly more to it. And how could I turn down any book?

Still, I was reluctant to take it. It said "Another Testament of Jesus Christ" right on the cover. Dave's attempt to share his religion was exactly the sort of thing Rabbi Singer had warned us against. And what would my mother think?

"Okay," I replied, "thanks for your book." I hesitated. "You know I'm a Jew, right?" I said, only half-teasing. " I don't believe in Jesus."

Dave nodded. "No pressure, man," he said. "You've definitely shown curiosity about our religion, though, and having this book will give you a chance to learn about it on your own."

Torn over what to do, it wasn't the book that made up my mind—it was my friendship with Dave. I remember thinking that Dave was the sort of person who would light Chanukah candles with me if I invited him. I wanted to show him the same respect.

"Okay," I said. "I'm cool with that. I like to study things out for myself."

I took the book from him. I stuck it in my backpack. And then I snuck it home, hiding it like contraband.

◇ ◻ ◇

Having taken the Book of Mormon didn't make it any easier for me to decide what to do with it.

It was just a book. Just a book from a friend. But there were so many relationships tied in that book already.

I couldn't give it back to Dave because I could tell from the way he'd given it to me that the book meant a lot to him. He'd gone out on a limb to give it to me; he and Shea had both taken time to prepare this specific copy for me. Even at a glance, I could see how they'd used a rainbow of colored pencils to highlight passages that spoke to specific questions I'd raised. I could see they'd put so much work into it, and I didn't want to let them down.

At the same time, though, I couldn't just leave it on my desk in my room, because sooner or later my mom would find it. I didn't know how she'd react, but I didn't want to disappoint her.

I remembered how supportive she'd been as I prepared to officially become a son of the commandments. A friend's mom had walked up to my mom after the service. "Jan, Jason gave the best bar mitzvah sermon I've ever heard," the woman said. "Have you thought about him becoming a rabbi? He would be incredible."

My mom beamed with pride. Her son, a rabbi. She knew I was serious about our religion. Or at least she hoped I was—and always would be.

I already knew she worried, on some level, about what it meant for a Jewish kid to live as a member of a minority, with mostly non-Jewish friends. She'd known Shea since we were twelve and was glad I had friends with good values, but when she found out he wasn't coming to my bar mitzvah, her first reaction was to suggest that maybe he didn't support me in my Judaism. I'd explained that it wasn't that at all—he'd just be out of town that day—but I knew the worry about whether friends would support me was still there.

What would she think if she found me reading this book? How would it change the way she saw me? Would it change the way she saw my friends, the trust she was willing to give them?

I didn't really want to find out. Since I wasn't willing to give the Book of Mormon back to my friends or to keep it in my house, it was exiled to a space between. I shoved it down under some books in my backpack, deep enough to stay out of sight at home but still within arm's reach if I ever decided what to do with it. But I put off that decision for long enough that the book practically became a part of my backpack. Long enough for it to get jostled, bent, and sometimes crushed by the heavy textbooks I buried it under every day.

It stayed there long enough that I almost quit thinking about it. I forgot about it just enough that one day, when we were working on some homework at lunch, I didn't think about where the book was at all when Dave offered to get my Social Studies notebook out of my backpack for me.

As he rooted through all the papers and books a teenager like me could cram into a backpack, he noticed the frayed blue cover and bent pages of his holy book. His face fell. "Jason, this may not be your scripture, but to me this book is the word of God," he said. "Please don't treat it this way."

◇ ▢ ◇

The more I thought about it, the more bitter I felt about Dave's comment.

He didn't understand. He didn't have a clue what he was asking of me. I couldn't keep it in my room. I couldn't risk my mom finding it.

Why had he even given it to me? I didn't want it. I never asked for it. I just wanted to debate religion. I didn't want his Christian, missionary book.

Why had he even given it to me? We both knew it wasn't just so I could learn a thing or two about Mormons. He was a future missionary: he wasn't just handing me a reference work. He was hoping, on some level at least, for something to happen. Hoping the book would reach me somehow. Change me.

But I had plans. I had goals. I had already made a commitment to my religion, a commitment to God: the change he doubtless wished for me couldn't be further from what I wanted for myself.

How dare he be so disappointed? Sure, my backpack had been rough on the book. But it's not like I had thrown it away or destroyed it.

I could have destroyed it.

I could destroy it.

I started working on a plan. Obviously, just throwing it in the garbage was out. That would raise questions. I would have to get rid of it in a way no one would find afterwards. Find a way to "lose" it without the risk of it ever coming back.

I waited until it got late one night. It was in the fall. It was dark outside. I slipped a lighter from the kitchen cupboard into my pocket—probably the same lighter we used to light Chanukah candles. With the Book of Mormon tucked under my shirt, I snuck out to the backyard. Went to an out-of-the-way spot between the garage and the white stucco fence between our house and the neighbors. The ground here was covered in gravel.

It wasn't the most elegant solution, but it would do. I could be rid of the book and the uncomfortable, conflicted feelings that came with it. I took the book out, fumbled with the lighter.

But just as I was about to flick the switch to start up the flames, I felt a voice, at once firm and gentle, pierce my mind and heart. "Do not burn my book," it said.

I hesitated. Was my mind playing tricks on me? Or was God really speaking?

I shook off the thought. Was I going to fall for this fake Mormon propaganda the same way I was ready to listen to "Mitch," the fake Jews-for-Jesus missionary? I held up the lighter again.

But that feeling of a voice pressed again. "Go to your room and read my book," it seemed to say.

I hesitated again. How would I feel if Dave burned the Torah scroll from which I had chanted for my bar mitzvah? I couldn't imagine him doing anything like that, but I knew that Christians had made a show of burning Jewish books before.

I couldn't let myself do something remotely similar. Burning a book, even if it was not wholly true, was wrong. And if there was any chance this voice, and this book, came from my God—the God of Abraham, Isaac, and Jacob—I might as well read it and settle the question for myself once and for all.

I put the lighter away and snuck the book back inside to read.

CHAPTER THREE

THE BOOK

◇

I read by the light of my lamp. Like a little kid staying up past his bedtime, I figured lamplight would be less likely to attract attention and easier to turn off if someone did happen to come by.

I had only gotten as far as the title page when I realized the Book of Mormon was no ordinary book. The book, the prophet Moroni says, "is to show unto the remnant of the house of Israel what great things the Lord hath done for their fathers; and that they may know the covenants of the Lord, that they are not cast off forever." Not only was I surprised to find myself addressed as a member of the house of Israel: I was surprised to find this book overtly arguing that God had not abandoned his covenant with us.

Rabbi Singer had not prepared me for this.

In almost the same breath, however, the Book of Mormon challenged my beliefs. The next phrase said the book was written "to the convincing of Jew and Gentile that Jesus is the Christ, the Eternal God." It was an uncomfortable proposition. I'd debated plenty with Shea and Dave whether Jesus might be the Christ, the Messiah, foretold in the Tanakh. I wasn't aware of anything in Jewish tradition or scripture, however, to support the notion that the Messiah—or any other human— might somehow be God.

If I'd just been part of an interfaith conversation with my friends, that would be an interesting difference to note. But I wasn't just in an interfaith conversation anymore. The book itself was addressing me, asking me to believe things. Experiencing scripture was more than just reading a book: it meant wrestling with it.

In the weeks that followed, I often stayed up late at night, still reading by lamplight, to study the prophets in the book and puzzle through the challenge their stories and teachings presented. The book's fundamental claim of Jesus as a divine Messiah was not something I accepted. And yet, the Book of Mormon kept surprising and engaging me.

It dealt with themes of exile and promise, of chosenness and suffering in ways that spoke to me. As a Jew, old promises about the land and the fruit of the vine still passed over my lips in prayer. Stories of what our people had been through had soaked deep into my sense of self. The land of Israel, both in the Biblical past and our collective present, loomed large in my community.

So in the beginning of the Book of Mormon, when Lehi and his family leave Jerusalem just before the invasion of Judea by the Babylonians, I cared about their plight. I knew about the Exile in Babylon, which was when deported Israelites who chose to worship their God far from their land profoundly shaped the future of Judaism as we know it. The people in the Book of Mormon felt like lost cousins on some parallel track.

Unlike the longing of the Jews for their lost homeland during the Babylonian exile, though, the spiritual leaders of Lehi's group seemed content never to physically return to Jerusalem. To accept a new land of promise instead. Their simultaneous faithfulness to the covenant and willingness to let a new place become holy intrigued me.

I also was really intrigued by 2 Nephi. In Judaism, we read a passage from the Torah, which contains the five books of Moses, each week. After the Torah portion, we read the *haftarah*, a passage from the prophets or later writings, often one that relates to the week's Torah portion in some way. During my bar mitzvah, for example, the *haftarah* was from 1 Samuel, and dealt with Samuel trying to talk the people out of choosing a king. I knew the prophet Isaiah from the *haftarah* and loved finding out that Nephi was interested in creating a commentary for his people on Isaiah, the same way Jews in exile had created commentaries to help people raised away from the land of Israel make sense of our sacred texts.

I already knew Rabbi Singer's interpretations of Isaiah. Nephi's interpretations were both similar and different. As a prophet, he said he'd seen the future of his people in a vision. He expressed concern about their suffering. He foresaw times they would regress into a "lost and fallen state." He said a day of restoration would come for all of scattered Israel. But Nephi argued that Jesus, a Messiah who would come before the next destruction of Jerusalem, would be the one true Messiah. Jews in that future exile, Nephi wrote, "need not look forward any more for a Messiah to come, for there should not any come, save it should be a false Messiah which should deceive the people; for there is save one Messiah spoken of by the prophets" (see 2 Nephi 25:18).

Most Jewish interpretations of Isaiah say that the "first time" God restored his people from a lost and fallen state was after the Exodus from Egypt, when they were brought to Mount Sinai to enter a holy and eternal covenant with him. The idolatry of Egypt, the spiritual malnourishment of being in slavery, the lack of prophetic teachings for centuries—all this contributed to the Jewish people's "lost and fallen state" during the Egyptian captivity, until Moses led them out of that state into a redemption.

Similarly, in Nephi's view, the Book of Mormon and its

testimony of Jesus Christ would "restore" the Jewish people and the other scattered remnants of the House of Israel, to the heights of spiritual purity and righteousness they found when they made that collective covenant with God on Mount Sinai. Nephi didn't think that the Sinai covenant would lose its significance when the Messiah came. Instead, Nephi seemed to view an eventual Jewish embrace of Jesus as a "restoration" of Jewish holiness and covenant renewal, not an abandonment of Judaism in favor of a totally new religion.

Another passage highlighted how Nephi's belief that Jesus would come as the Messiah would go hand in hand with his continued concern for the future of the Jewish people. Nephi recorded the Nephites as keeping the law of Moses. He clearly loved the Torah and the prophets whose writings he had. And he emphasized that God would care about the Jews long after Jesus' coming: "O ye Gentiles, have ye remembered the Jews, mine ancient covenant people?" God's voice asked in one of Nephi's prophecies. "Nay; but ye have cursed them, and have hated them, and have not sought to recover them. But behold, I will return all these things upon your own heads; for I the Lord have not forgotten my people" (2 Nephi 29:5).

As I continued to study the Book of Mormon, I learned that Jesus himself spoke about the continued role Jews would play in sacred history:

> And because I said unto you that old things have passed away, I do not destroy that which hath been spoken concerning things which are to come. *For behold, the covenant which I have made with my people is not all fulfilled*; but the law which was given unto Moses hath an end in me (3 Nephi 15:7–8; italics added).

That reference to a continuing covenant mattered to me. It had been hard for me to consider a Christian Messiah who abandoned his people, but the Book of Mormon depicted Jesus as maintaining a relationship with the house of Israel, expressly including both Jews and scattered descendants of Jacob in the Americas and wherever they might be.

Somewhere in my reading, without quite realizing what was happening, I found myself wrestling against the text less and absorbing it more. I know the Book of Mormon doesn't speak to everyone, but it spoke to questions I'd been asking before I started talking religion with Shea and Dave. It felt like the book had found me.

The Book of Mormon's Jesus showed me everything I was looking for in a Messiah. I perceived his transcendent power as well as his immanent presence in the world, in the life of the Jewish people, and by extension in my own life. Reading the book, I began to feel the same hope as Dave and Shea that Jesus was real and would come again to fulfill the rest of the Messianic prophecies. He would be lion as well as lamb. He had not forgotten his people.

I wasn't sure yet what to make of that hope. What I wanted from Jesus would be a "restoration" of Jewish holiness and covenant renewal, not a conversion to a new religion. Still, the Book of Mormon was like a Middle Testament for me, a bridge between the emphases of the Tanakh and the claims of the Christian New Testament (a book I had not yet read). I was intrigued by it. I was annoyed by it. Sometimes I was deeply moved by it.

It was early one morning when I got to the last chapter of the Book of Mormon and read a passage Dave had highlighted for me. In Moroni 10:3–5, the last prophet of the Book of Mormon addresses readers and says we should think back on history, reflect on God's relationship with humanity, and then pray to know the truth. By the power of the Holy Ghost, the scripture says, we can know the truth of all things.

I had to know. A part of me was nervous to know, but I had to know. I knelt down to pray, something I had seen Shea and Dave do in their family prayers.

There are moments in life that transcend the limits of our

understanding. Moments that fill the heart, enlarge the soul. Moments when God writes his will on us, when the flesh of our hearts becomes his tablet.

I found myself closing my prayer in the name of Jesus Christ. The next moment, I was filled from the crown of my head to the soles of my feet with the spirit of God. I felt full of light. Like I was glowing with it.

When I rose from my prayer, I knew for myself that the Book of Mormon was true.

◇ ◻ ◇

It was around five in the morning, but I needed to talk with someone. I decided to call Dave. "Dave," I said when he answered groggily, "I know it's true."

"What's true, Jason?" he asked, still sounding disoriented.

"The Book of Mormon you gave me."

That shook him all the way awake. "Wait, what! You read the Book of Mormon?" Dave asked. "No wonder you've gotten so quiet about things."

"It's true, man," I continued, tears streaming down my cheeks. "I read the promise from Moroni that you highlighted and decided to ask God if it's true. I felt it. The Book of Mormon is just as true as my Bible is."

Dave couldn't believe it.

He later confided in me that, at the time, he didn't feel as sure it was true as I did. He admitted he felt a little jealous that he didn't have the clear conversion experience I'd had. My experience motivated him to do more on his own. "Jason," he said when he'd gone through his own process, "when you told me that you received an answer from God that the book was true, I wanted an answer too. So, I started studying and praying more earnestly and I felt God telling me, 'You already know this is true.'"

He realized then that spiritual experience isn't a competition. God gave me what I needed: a dramatic revelation to prepare me for the obstacles on the path he was calling me to. Dave needed the steady, gentle reassurance he got to remind him that faith usually grows like a person, in ways you'd never notice from day to day but are apparent when you look back over the years.

In any case, Dave was there for me when I needed him. He'd been there for me in our religious discussions. He'd gone out on a limb to give me a Book of Mormon I sometimes resented him for sharing. And he was ready to take me further after God spoke to me through that book.

One thing I was really curious about after praying about the Book of Mormon was Joseph Smith. The Book of Mormon only includes the story of Joseph getting the plates to translate and briefly mentions visits from the angel Moroni. It's kind of a weird way, frankly, to be introduced to the modern history of the faith.

"So what is it with this Joseph Smith guy?" I asked Dave. "Do you really consider him a prophet? What does that mean? A prophet like Moses?"

"Exactly a prophet like Moses," Dave replied.

Hm. "What made him a prophet?" I asked.

True to form, Dave decided to let me sort some things out for myself and got me some reading in the form of a pamphlet about Joseph Smith, which related the story of his early life and first vision. It was a really simple, thin text—which was great, because it made it a lot easier to hide in my backpack.

I wish people who grew up as Latter-day Saints, always knowing this story, could feel what it was like for me to learn about Joseph Smith. When I first read Joseph's words, I felt so connected to his experience. His openness and authenticity about his challenges. His struggle to know which church was right, the confusion over the various doctrines taught in his day. I came from a totally different time, place, and background, but I realized I felt a lot like Joseph. I'd been born between different versions of the truth; sometimes I felt torn between them.

Who was right—or were they all wrong together?

For me, Mormonism was something different than just choosing Christianity over Judaism. The sense I had gotten from Mormonism is that it found something missing in both Judaism and mainstream Christianity.

Joseph Smith immediately felt to me like a prophet. A modern prophet. I thought back on the Torah portion I'd read at my bar mitzvah, about Korach's rebellion against Moses. I'd worried then and since about rebelling against the prophets, but I hadn't thought as much about how much courage it might take to identify, accept, and follow a prophet in my own era.

I thought about what Joseph Smith had said about his vision:

> Though I was hated and persecuted for saying that I had seen a vision, yet it was true; and while they were persecuting me, reviling me, and speaking all manner of evil against me falsely for so saying, I was led to say in my heart: Why persecute me for telling the truth? I have actually seen a vision; and who am I that I can withstand God, or why does the world think to make me deny what I have actually seen? For I had seen a vision; I knew it, and I knew that God knew it, and I could not deny it, neither dared I do it; at least I knew that by so doing I would offend God, and come under condemnation (Joseph Smith—History 1:25).

I realized that Joseph's words could apply just as well to my experience gaining a testimony of the Book of Mormon: "I knew it, and I knew that God knew it, and I could not deny it." Those words rang true in the core of my soul.

I held on to those words as I began to think through the implications of my experience. The Book of Mormon made clear that following Jesus involved getting baptized and that, like the gates of heaven opening on Yom Kippur, baptism led to a forgiveness of sins.

In Jewish history, though, the word *baptism* did not have positive connotations. There had been forced baptisms of Jews at some points in history. There had been other times when baptism, though not forced, had been required to reduce discrimination and get a chance at full participation in social life. For many Jews, baptism was a symbol of the death of a Jewish life, the breaking of a line of legacy. But if there was truth buried beneath the historical misuse of the principle, I needed to be baptized.

This time I called Shea.

"I wanted to tell you I've been reading the Book of Mormon that Dave gave me," I began.

"Wow," Shea said. "I didn't think you would actually read it. What do you think?"

I took a deep breath. "Well, I believe it. I know it's true. And I feel I need to be baptized for forgiveness of my sins."

The phone got quiet for a second. "You have got to be kidding me," Shea said. "Is this for real?"

"It's real," I said. "I've really been reading the Book of Mormon. And I want you to baptize me."

"Wow . . ." Shea said again. "I would be honored to. I can't believe it." He hesitated. "One thing though. Since you're only 15 years old, you would need your parents' permission."

My heart sank. That wasn't what I had in mind. "Why would I need my parents' permission?" I asked. "Let's just go to the lake tomorrow and you can baptize me in secret." Since all I really knew about baptism came from the Book of Mormon, getting baptized secretly in a lake felt totally reasonable to me.[1]

"Jason," Shea said, "it doesn't work like that. You need to become an official member of The Church of Jesus Christ of Latter-day Saints."

"I don't know about that," I admitted. "I was thinking I

---

1. In the book of Mosiah, a group of people do exactly this (see Mosiah 18).

could remain a Jew and just be secretly baptized, so that I can be forgiven of my sins and follow Jesus in my heart." It would be a much bigger deal for me to stop attending synagogue services and start going to Church with Shea and Dave. That would definitely upset my parents. And honestly, it wasn't really something I wanted. Just because I believed in the Book of Mormon version of Jesus now didn't mean I wanted to be separated from Judaism and the Jewish community.

Shea said, "Part of being baptized is taking upon yourself the name of Jesus Christ and becoming a member of his church."

Now it was my turn to say "wow" and let the news sink in. "Uh, I didn't realize it worked that way," I said. "I guess I'll have to find a way to talk to my parents about this."

"I'll be praying for you," Shea said. Then, to avoid any more surprises, he talked me through the logistics of the conversion process. If I got my parents' permission to be baptized, he explained, I would need to meet with the missionaries, take lessons, make spiritual and moral commitments.

"Cool," I said, trying to keep my cool even as I said it. "I'd love to meet with the missionaries."

What to do, what to do? Part of me wanted to run away from the whole thing. After what I'd felt as I prayed, though, it felt too late. There was no going back now, no simple way to ignore this.

And I didn't want to back down from baptism. If I had to have a conversation with my parents about baptism, so be it, even if I was totally intimidated by the idea.

I got to work right away putting it off.

It was so much easier to imagine a secret baptism with Shea than to think through the drama that would go along with changing religions. Belief notwithstanding, I just couldn't imagine a life where I would be going to church every Sunday and assuming a Mormon identity. Religion is belief, but it's not only belief. It's what people call you, it's where you feel like you belong, it's the stories that fill your imagination and the hopes you have for the future. Moved as I was by the Book of Mormon, I still thought of myself as a Jew. I imagined I would continue my Jewish life as usual: live the Torah, learn with the rabbis, marry under a chuppah, circumcise my sons, plant trees in the land of Israel. How could I turn my back on my people, my family? How could I join this other people, this people whose exodus story ended not in the land of Israel but in the mountains of Utah?

And yet, how could I do anything else?

I finally decided at least one thing for sure. I needed to tell my mom about my desire to get baptized first. She was the parent over religion, just like my dad was the parent over sports. She deserved a chance to process it first. And if she said "no," that would be okay, at least God would know that I had tried.

I finally worked up the courage to talk to her and found a moment to come clean. We were sitting together in the kitchen after school. No one else was home. Just me and my mom.

"Mom," I said, "I need to tell you something."

She looked at me with a mix of care and concern. "What is it, honey?"

"I've been reading the Book of Mormon," I admitted.

CHAPTER FOUR

NEITHER WITH
YOU ONLY

◇

In the Book of Deuteronomy, Moses calls the children of Israel together and addresses them. At one point, he says:

> Ye stand this day all of you before the Lord your God; your captains of your tribes, your elders, and your officers, with all the men of Israel, Your little ones, your wives, and thy stranger that is in thy camp. . . . That he may establish thee to day for a people unto himself, and that he may be unto thee a God, as he hath said unto thee, and as he hath sworn unto thy fathers, to Abraham, to Isaac, and to Jacob. Neither with you only do I make this covenant and this oath; but with him that standeth here with us this day before the Lord our God, and also with him that is not here with us this day (See Deut 29: 10, 13–15).

Jewish tradition says that not all that Moses was taught was written down. Additional details were passed down orally through the Seventy Elders and to the next prophet, Joshua, and down through the generations, from prophet to prophet, and from elder to elder, from rabbi to rabbi. Some of this information was later written in stories called *midrashim*. One midrash, commenting on this passage in Deuteronomy explains that the scripture says "him that is not here with us this day" because Moses included all future Jews in his statement. The midrash further states that the souls of all the Jews who would ever live gathered at the revelation on Sinai.[1]

When I told my mother that I had been reading the Book of Mormon, she didn't just react as any mother might, with understandable concern about a new influence in her son's life. She reacted as someone concerned with continuing thousands of years of tradition. As someone, perhaps, who felt the unseen spiritual tug of an ancient moment on Mount Sinai.

She was visibly upset. "Who gave it to you?" she demanded.

"Dave," I told her. "From school."

"Why did he give it to you?" she asked in frustration.

I shrugged. "Because we've been talking about differences between Christianity and Judaism. I've been interested in the topic ever since Rabbi Singer came to the synagogue."

"Dave shouldn't have given you that book," she said.

"Well, why not?" I asked. I realized I needed to get the rest out quickly. It was no good if we fought over the fact that I had the book in the first place and didn't get to the hardest part. "I've read it and I believe it's true," I confessed. "I believe Jesus is the Messiah and that I need to be baptized. Can I have your permission?"

She looked at me like she could hardly believe what I was saying. "Absolutely not," she snapped. "I'm really upset about your Mormon friends trying to convert you."

It wasn't right for them to take the blame. This was my choice. "I approached them first," I said. "I wanted to find out why they believe Jesus is the Messiah." Hadn't she heard me say that this had all started in our synagogue? I tried again. "I was curious because of the Rabbi Singer event at Hebrew High."

---

1. See Midrash Tanhuma, Nitzavim 3

I was trying to be calm and reasonable, but tension filled the air. I knew this was hard on my mother. I understood why she would want to push blame over onto someone else, but I wished she'd also be willing to listen to me and take what I'd experienced seriously enough to let it make a difference in my life.

But that's a lot to ask a mother. She gave me what she could in the moment instead. "I want you to study more with the rabbis," she said, "so that you'll think straight about this."

I nodded. That was a peace offering I could give without the slightest hint of regret. "Sure," I promised her. "I would love to study more with the rabbis. I love the Torah and the Bible. I would love to learn more about Judaism."

◇ ▢ ◇

So we had a deal. Once a week, my mom would take me to a Torah study group at our local, Reform congregation. That was how I'd show my respect for our faith and the gift of tradition she'd given me.

It was kind of awkward, though: it was all adults and I was the only teenager. The discussion followed the weekly Torah portion reading and tended to be a little general for my interest. Despite having other commitments with school sports and social life, I was willing to give it a shot. Pretty soon, though, my mom decided that it wasn't going to work. This wasn't reaching me deeply enough: I needed a more rigorous approach to Torah study.

She wasn't one to give up on something that mattered so much to her. At Passover, Jews review the advice of ancient rabbis about how to teach children. It all depends on the type of children you have, the rabbis say. They talk about four types: one who is wise, one who is wicked, one who is simple, and one who does not know how to ask a question.

My mother had seen how deeply I could study. An inability to ask questions was certainly not the problem. If anything, she probably felt like I'd gotten into this situation to begin with by asking too many questions! And I wasn't really a simple answer person. Discussion that was calibrated to the attention level of a mixed group never seemed to satisfy me. To her credit, she didn't treat me as the wicked or rebellious child who needs a clear rebuke. She treated me as the wise child. At the Passover seder each year, we reviewed how the wise child asks specific and detailed questions and ought to be taught with specific and detailed answers, withholding nothing, down to the finest point of the law. And so it was that my mother arranged for me to take one-on-one lessons from Rabbi Raphael.

I'd met Rabbi Raphael at Hebrew High classes in our synagogue, where he taught courses on Jewish thought and Jewish ethics in love and relationships. For our classes, though, my mom would drive me down to the Phoenix Community Kollel, an Orthodox center for learning, with about 6 full-time rabbis who led both worship and Torah study.

I had never been in an Orthodox shul before, but when my mom took me to meet with Rabbi Raphael for the first time, I felt at home. All four walls were full to bursting with books, some on top of one another: disorderly, disorganized, as if someone had been right in the middle of reading all of them at once, always finding an urgent reason to check something in the next before properly putting back the first.

Most were in Aramaic or Hebrew. Multiple versions of the Talmud. Commentaries upon commentaries upon commentaries. Their library had kabbalistic, or mystical, works intended only for advanced study, after age forty, once you'd had time to master "the basics" of Torah and Talmud. Looking around the shelves, I felt like Harry Potter walking into Hogwarts for the first time. I wanted to read everything. I wanted the rabbi to teach me what was in all those books, and to help me understand them.

The building that housed all those books was simple and unassuming. The classrooms were very basic, almost like meeting rooms in a library. Who needed amenities when you had so many books? The ark where their Torah scroll was kept was very simple, with none of the ornate decorations communities often use to honor the Torah. Their offering instead was study of the *halakhah* and the *aggadah*, the commandments and the teachings, contained within the holy books. They lived by a motto from our prayer book: "the study of the Torah is equal to them all [the other commandments], because it leads to them all."[2]

There was a little of eastern Europe left in that place. Sometimes the rabbis would speak in Yiddish. Sometimes I'd catch the nostalgic scent of Ashkenazi Jewish foods like gefilte fish. Most of the rabbis there had roots in New York but had moved to Phoenix to support the small but growing modern Orthodox community there.

In addition to being well-read, Rabbi Raphael was a *tzaddik*, a righteous and saintly man. I don't know what my mother told him or left out about why I was there. He never brought it up: it always felt like he just wanted to teach me and I just wanted to learn. Really learn. I wanted to be taken seriously as a student of religion, of Torah. And Rabbi Raphael took me very seriously. I never felt like he was sidestepping my spiritual questions with secular answers. He believed all those four walls of books had the answers I was searching for. I just needed to give him, and the accumulation of millennia of Torah wisdom, a chance.

I still felt the power of my spiritual experience with the Book of Mormon. But not for a moment did I think that negated his learning and wisdom, that it reduced the value of the treasures of insight he had access to.

I believed he had a very deep well of living water. And I was very, very thirsty. We began with the creation and Eden and inched our way forward, wrestling with questions of God's

---

2. Talmud Bavli, Shabbat 127a.

intent for humankind, and of what it means in particular to have a Jewish soul.

◇ ▢ ◇

At the same time I was studying with Rabbi Raphael, I was continuing to study the Book of Mormon and the restored gospel. I was also going to Hebrew High, a once-a-week evening where you could talk classes on Jewish thought and culture or Hebrew language. And of course, Shea and Dave were open for religious discussions. I could learn. I could talk. All that was left was to decide what to do about it all!

At the end of my sophomore year, I tried going on a date with a Mormon girl. It's one thing to believe in a faith. It's another to imagine yourself in a community. Without saying anything, I wanted to get a sense of what it might be like to have a relationship with a Latter-day Saint. Our single date, though, mostly felt awkward. At the time, I got the impression that she was nervous about dating a non-member—though maybe she just wasn't interested in me! I still felt out of place. Like I was on the edge of a world I didn't quite understand.

One evening at Hebrew High, during a break between classes, I ended up flirting with an old friend instead. I'd been at her bat mitzvah, and we'd sung in choir together after Shea got me to join, but sometimes the way you see someone just suddenly changes. I asked her if she wanted to go to the next play at the high school. She said yes. We talked and joked on the way there. It was outside, so we were sitting on the grass, and by the end of the play she was leaning against me. Pretty soon we were dating. As it happened, she was good friends with Shea's girlfriend, who was also Mormon and also in the choir. That meant that my girlfriend and I ended up going on lots of double dates with Shea and his girlfriend.

On my own, I spent a lot of time with Shea, Dave, and later with Shea's cousin, Matt Nelson, who was also a Latter-day

Saint. Religion wasn't the only thing, or even the main thing, we'd talk about. It also meant a lot to me to know they were my friends: friends who would support me in making good choices, who would share the treasure of their faith with me but would also support me even if I never ended up getting baptized.

I'd go over sometimes to Shea's house. On one visit, I noticed his dad had a big collection of Latter-day Saint books. It wasn't the Phoenix Community Kollel, to be sure, but there were volumes and volumes of scholarship and commentaries. He must've had a whole shelf just by Hugh Nibley. I stared at them, like a kid at a candy store window.

Shea saw I was interested and let me borrow some: including some, it turned out, that were out of print or signed by the author. Apparently, he forgot to tell his dad, who noticed books going missing and then reappearing one by one. Shea's dad was excited to see those books he treasured getting read. One day, he started talking to his sons about the books, hoping to have a good discussion. When neither Shea nor any of his brothers could follow the conversation, his dad finally asked, "Well, if you're not reading my books, who is?"

"Jason," Shea said.

His dad was a little nervous at first that before even being baptized, I was diving so deep into Mormon thought and debate, but then he remembered how hungry for knowledge I was and decided it was all right. He and I ended up having some good talks. The ability to think deeply about the new doctrines I had absorbed played an important role in growing and strengthening my faith.

One weekend during the beginning of my junior year, my parents happened to be out of town and I decided to sleep over at Shea's on Saturday night and then go to Church with the Owens family on Sunday. I remember playing Risk the night before and feeling my excitement rising. I knew the Book of Mormon was true, I knew the Church was true, but I'd never been before. What would it be like?

I'll admit to having some negative preconceived notions about Christian meetings. Even symbols like the cross can be hard for Jews: for centuries, people have blamed us for Jesus' crucifixion, sometimes attacking Jewish communities out of "revenge." On a more contemporary note, I was put off by my impression that many school friends' church services were a kind of Christian entertainment, complete with rock bands, energetic preachers, and coffee shops attached to their worship space. When it came to God, I didn't want to be convinced to pay attention: I wanted serious worship that took my commitment for granted.

As we got ready for church in the morning, I couldn't wait to see what even just the building was like. I wasn't disappointed. I saw a clean, organized, family-centered atmosphere. With no crosses! That was a relief for me.

I appreciated how simple the classrooms and chapel were. Kind of like the Kollel, actually. I did a little people-watching, taking in how focused on relationships and family the members were. And then the meeting started.

The prayers were from the heart, spoken rather than chanted, and just made up on the spot. I was shocked people could pray whatever they wanted and the Bishop just let it happen. After some announcements, young men my age and even younger blessed and passed the sacrament. I didn't think I should take it until I was baptized, but I was glued to the solemnity of the ordinance. Part of me wished again that Shea could just go baptize me in the nearest place with water so I could take the bread and water and participate in their echo of the baptismal covenant.

I was amazed by the beautiful voices of regular members in the pews. I knew Shea could sing incredibly well, but people without his talent seemed willing and able to sing with emotion and clarity. And I liked listening to the words of the hymns.

It was the first week of the month when I went. I don't think anybody's description could have kept me from being surprised at how unstructured and yet also authentic that first fast and testimony meeting was. I was used to rabbis sharing a sermon based on a passage, maybe helping talk us through some nuance of the Hebrew as they analyzed a line or principle in English. I really appreciated a lot of the insights I'd gained that way. I enjoyed Jewish services.

My first impression of Latter-day Saint worship wasn't that it was better or worse so much as really different. Here, people just got up and shared really personal stuff. I wasn't used to that at all. I felt the Spirit as many spoke. And I felt this reassuring sense that the members were really committed to what they believed. They clearly weren't attending this church because it was the most entertaining or sophisticated, but because it was true. Because they knew it was the place God wanted them to be.

Since then, I've heard plenty of people say you shouldn't go to church just for the people. But that first time, the people made a big impression on me. I was impressed by everyone's humility and desire to support one another. And when I went to priests' quorum with Shea, I thought it was amazing how religious the young men were. Their parents and teachers might have felt differently, but from my perspective, they seemed really knowledgeable about their religion. Maybe it's the culture of giving everyone callings, but Latter-day Saints seem to have a higher average working knowledge of their faith at the same time there are fewer genuine experts.

And I thought it was awesome that young men, my age, could bless the Sacrament and baptize people. That they could really exercise Priesthood authority. I wanted that. I wanted to be part of that brotherhood more than anything. I wanted to belong here.

That desire to belong raised hard questions. When I first asked about being baptized, Shea had made clear that it wasn't something I could do in secret as a sign of internal conviction. Baptism would mean visibly exterior changes to my life and associations. I'd be going to Latter-day Saint services with no cantor sharing the music that resonated so deeply with me, no Hebrew to help me learn concepts from an older worldview, no Torah scroll to pass down and honor. No oneg or kiddush spread out for people to nosh on after services while they talked. It would be a different kind of experience, with its own distinct draw and beauty.

I had a testimony of the restored gospel. If I'd been braver, or had a clearer idea of how things worked, I could have stood up on that first day to share it. But knowing I believed was not the same as imagining myself more or less exclusively committed to the life of a Latter-day Saint.

As moving as it had been, going to Church once didn't make it easier to imagine myself into that Latter-day Saint life. My studies with Rabbi Raphael were going well. Hebrew High was going well. My relationship with my girlfriend was going well. Would it be so hard to just keep living the life I'd been raised for, the life I'd chosen for myself at age thirteen?

How much was I willing to give up for the sake of one book that had spoken to my soul?

CHAPTER FIVE

SNEAKING OUT AND COMING CLEAN

◇

One of the ways my dad showed he cared about me was by always taking time to toss around a ball. That was his language, and I learned it fluently. By high school, I was on the football team, the baseball team, the wrestling team.

And so I knew a thing or two about what was going on with my peers at school, how many of them were sneaking out of their parents' houses at night to go get drunk, have sex, make all the impulsive choices so many teenagers seize to feel grown-up without having to bother yet with maturity.

I snuck out, too. Just once. To go to early morning seminary.

At the beginning of my senior year, I'd made it there once after staying the night at Shea's. I can't remember how much I learned in one class session, but the idea of seminary really spoke to me. I felt a lot of respect for Brother Rizley, the early morning seminary teacher. They happened to be studying the Book of Mormon that year. That wasn't something I could get anywhere else.

I knew that it wouldn't be realistic to go all the time, but

I loved studying the Book of Mormon. So one morning, I just decided to go for it. I woke up early, put pillows under my blanket in case anyone in my family poked their head into my room, and snuck out to class. I longed so much to understand the Book of Mormon better, to grasp how I could apply its teachings in my life.

How much was I willing to do for the sake of one book that spoke to my soul?

Even just attending two sessions, I could tell many of the students in seminary were thinking about how they would use what they were learning as missionaries. Caught up in the exhilaration of my forbidden attendance, I had the thought that I would love to serve a mission one day. What a twist! What would Rabbi Singer think if he could see me now—having gone from studying his website for ways to counter missionary arguments to longing to learn about how to be a missionary from a Latter-day Saint early morning seminary class?

One day, I quietly asked Dave Thaxton about who could even go. "Are new converts supposed to go on missions like you guys?" I said.

Dave nodded solemnly. "Jason, when you receive the Melchizedek Priesthood and are ordained an Elder of the Church, it is a commandment for all young men, including you, to serve a mission."

"Okay," I said. "Well, I'm not even baptized yet. We'll see."

But I felt the desire growing within me. Dave was bold and I responded to bold.

I hadn't grown up with the idea of a two-year gap in my plans, of course. I'd filled my own vague idea of the future with other half-formed thoughts. My girlfriend meant the world to me and I hadn't imagined myself leaving her for so long. Truth be told, I hadn't even told her how I felt about Mormonism. That might feel like a betrayal on its own, without the added twist of my new faith taking me away for two years.

And my romantic life wasn't the only concern. I really

looked up to Papa Al and his example of military service during World War II. The terrorist attacks on September 11th, at the beginning of my junior year, left me with fantasies of confronting our country's enemies. Before that, I'd loved the Constitution and thought about becoming a judge someday, but after 9/11, I started playing with the idea of attending the US Naval Academy and trying to become a Marine officer.

It felt like serving a two-year mission might affect all that. I wasn't sure how my girlfriend, let alone Uncle Sam, felt about an extended disappearance from regular life. I tried not to think too hard about it. Talking with Dave, though, I wanted to walk the path God set before me. Whatever effect it might have on my own ideas and dreams.

◇ ◻ ◇

By my junior year, a lot of my friends were starting to lose interest in Hebrew High. Some had probably been losing interest for a while: even freshman year, some of my friends talked me into switching from the "Great Jewish Thinkers" class I'd been going to for "Jews in the Media," so we could watch movies instead. As you get older and have more options for how to spend your time, though, it's easier to completely bail. For some people, having a bar mitzvah or bat mitzvah out of the way reduces the family pressure to attend. In any kind of learning, there's a temptation to learn enough to get by and then just let yourself plateau. About half of my peers had reached the point where they had all the Jewish knowledge they felt like they needed for their lives. Others kept reaching for more: I remember one friend in particular, Chad, who was really serious about his Judaism, who always seemed to want to know and internalize more. And I was still a sponge. My girlfriend would come sometimes, and I'd follow her to Hebrew language class. When she wasn't there, though, I gravitated more toward the classes on Jewish thought.

That fall, there happened to be a course at Hebrew High on "Jewish Response to Christian Missionaries." The timing, right as I was starting to wonder about a Mormon mission, was wild. I decided I had to check it out. I'm not sure quite what I wanted. It would have made my life simpler if someone could persuade me away from Mormonism, and maybe on some level I wondered if that would happen. On another level, though, I think it was just curiosity. So often, we live in one frame for seeing the world. The fish knows water; the bird knows air. Of course I was drawn to the chance to see something from two very different angles.

The difference I expected was between Dave Thaxton's missionary conviction and Jewish concern. Another striking difference in "Jewish Response to Christian Missionaries" turned out to be between two types of Jewish responses. The class had little in common with the approach I'd become obsessed with before. Rabbi Singer had taken a scriptural route, delving into the prophets and debating interpretations. This class focused instead on historical evidence. We talked about archeology and Roman-era sources, about conflicting details in the Chirstian gospels. The main argument turned out to be that Jesus may not have even been a historical figure at all.

For Latter-day Saints, my experience in Hebrew High watching movies with Jewish actors and talking about archeology might feel strange. The Church is so focused on the spiritual and doctrinal sides of religion, it can be hard to understand the cultural dimensions. Different aspects of religion are also mixed together, though, like different ingredients in the same soup. Religion may be old, but the way we experience it is shaped by far more recent choices about what to emphasize.

I didn't understand it at the time, but looking back, I can see how my experience growing up Jewish echoed the thought of two towering rabbis from the early twentieth century. The world is always changing, but most people in the early 1800s traveled, communicated, and worked in more or less the same ways people had for hundreds and even thousands of years. Railroads, steamships, telegraphs, and factories changed all that practically within a generation. As the sons of rabbis from Eastern Europe came to the United States in a wave of steam-powered immigration, they had to grapple with how to translate a way of living and thinking their ancestors had refined through long debates into a jarringly modern world. A world, furthermore, where research into evolution and the origins of the Bible's text called old assumptions into question, where mysticism and the supernatural were increasingly seen as superstition. Mordecai Kaplan and Joseph Soloveitchik approached that same problem in two distinct ways.

Kaplan, who published *Judaism as Civilization* in 1934, emphasized our history, language, values, and culture, while de-emphasizing supernatural beliefs. When rabbis at Hebrew High evaluated the rationality of a religion, they were echoing his approach. It wasn't all archeology and history, of course. Being a people involves shared stories, shared worldview, shared commitments. Overall, our rabbis did a wonderful job of giving us a strong sense of Jewish identity and values, and of helping us feel that we could be both Jewish and modern. They succeeded at Kaplan's goals. I felt part of a Jewish culture and civilization because of their work.

Soloveitchik, who was fourteen years younger than Kaplan but came from a similar background, also advocated for the combination of secular learning with religious thought. For Soloveitchik, though, the commandments—and the body of religious law, or *halakha* they had inspired—were central. You didn't ask whether those divine commandments were rational: you used rational inquiry to find new ways to follow them. His book *Halakhic Man* presented religious law as a grounding force in the modern world, a foundation for a balanced life in the here-and-now. That philosophy animated modern orthodox thinkers like Rabbi Singer and Rabbi Rafael. I had learned to love the life rhythms of the Torah in part because of their work.

Both those approaches, though, were designed to side-step the awkward question of the mystical. And it's on that mystical level that Mormonism had entered my life and psyche. I didn't care all that much whether historians had room for doubt about Jesus' existence and ministry. I cared about what had happened in my backyard and in my room reading by lamplight and in some hidden part of my soul. I cared about the story I felt God trying to tell me.

The class on Christian Mission at Hebrew High talked past my dilemma. I believed in the Book of Mormon and its particular witness of Jesus. They spoke to me for mystical and scriptural reasons, not for secular or historical ones. I could never trade that conviction for a thin helping of historical doubt. I was just as sure, though, that I could never, and would never wish to, abandon all my connection to Jewish identity and history. I needed to find a way to reconcile the parts of myself instead. Since I didn't know how to, all I could do was walk by faith, out into the darkness, trusting that if I did what was right to the best of my knowledge, God would lead me to a place of peace in the end. Whether in this world or a future, supernatural one, it didn't matter: both felt real to me. If anything, the unseen world felt realer.

I was almost finished with high school when I decided to talk openly with Rabbi Raphael about my beliefs. I had so much respect for him I'd been afraid at first to bring up the subject. But after studying with him long enough, I trusted him enough to be honest.

I did it with a book. Somewhere between the Book of Mormon and all the books in Shea's dad's library, I'd read the New Testament, and I finally worked up the courage to bring a copy with me to Torah study. I showed him Matthew 5:17–20:

> Think not that I am come to destroy the law, or the prophets:
> I am not come to destroy, but to fulfil. For verily I say unto

you, Till heaven and earth pass, one jot or one tittle shall
in no wise pass from the law, till all be fulfilled. Whosoever
therefore shall break one of these least commandments, and
shall teach men so, he shall be called the least in the kingdom of heaven: but whosoever shall do and teach them, the
same shall be called great in the kingdom of heaven. For I
say unto you, That except your righteousness shall exceed
the righteousness of the scribes and Pharisees, ye shall in no
case enter into the kingdom of heaven.

"Rabbi," I said, "I think Jesus is teaching here that the Torah
must be observed until heaven and earth pass away. All the
prophecies of the Messianic Age have not yet been fulfilled.
Heaven and earth have clearly not passed away. Is it possible to
follow the Torah and believe Jesus *will* be the Messiah?"

Rabbi Raphael's face did not betray the least shock or disappointment at my question. "It is good that Jesus is teaching
that the Torah is eternal, and we must keep it and not break it,"
he said. " I do not have a problem with you hoping that Jesus
will be the Messiah. But, since you were born a Jew, born into
the covenant of Abraham and Sinai, it is your duty to live the
Torah." Like it was for Soloveitchik, that obligation was central
and grounding for Rabbi Rafael.

Any tension I'd been holding eased out of my body. It felt
so good to be able to have an honest conversation, to share
what was on my mind without worrying about the emotional
repercussions. "Rabbi," I said, "I don't have any problem with
the Torah. But I find Jesus so compelling and I believe he will
be the Messiah. I believe he will be the one coming again to
save the Jewish people from our enemies."

Rabbi Raphael could have responded dismissively or de-
fensively. He didn't. Instead, he gave me some space to breathe,
considering what I said and choosing his answer carefully.
"Well, we can't know for sure that Jesus will be the Messiah,"
he said. "You hope he will be the Messiah, but you don't know
for sure, since he has not fulfilled the prophecies the Messiah

is to fulfill." He paused and looked right at me. "I will tell you this: when the Messiah comes and fulfills all the prophecies, I will ask him if it is his first or second time coming. If he says it is his second time, I will know you are right. If he says it is his first time, I am right. But, until that day comes, it is your duty in the covenant to live the Torah."

What a beautiful conversation—but what a frustrating answer! I was torn, as I saw it, between Torah and Gospel. Which was I to follow? Jesus lived the Torah, but Latter-day Saints live the Gospel.

◇ ◻ ◇

I didn't have a Latter-day Saint equivalent of a rabbi to turn to next. The Latter-day Saint system of calling laypeople to serve and teach alongside their other life responsibilities is a beautiful thing in many ways, but there were times I could have used someone who had devoted their life to study.

The closest thing I had were the prophets in the scriptures. As a counterpoint to Rabbi Raphael's recommendation to wait for the fulfillment of all the prophecies (including the resurrection of all the dead), I looked to the Book of Mormon prophet Jacob's confidence that Jesus, after coming first like a lamb, would fulfill the "lion" Messianic prophecies during his Second Coming. In his interpretation of Isaiah 11:11, Jacob says:

> And behold, according to the words of the prophet, the Messiah will set himself again the second time to recover them; wherefore, he will manifest himself unto them in power and great glory, unto the destruction of their enemies, when that day cometh when they shall believe in him; and none will he destroy that believe in him (2 Nephi 6:14).

For Jacob, it is this Messiah (curiously, Isaiah 11:11 says "the Lord" in the passage he quotes) who comes a "second time" to recover the Jewish people. In his Second Coming, he will manifest himself as a lion, destroying his people's enemies.

Fulfilling all the promises.

Rabbi Raphael wasn't wrong. We could wait until then, until every grace was opened and every unjust wound healed, to find out if Jesus is the Messiah. But if I longed for the Messiah, shouldn't I follow him now? Shouldn't I be willing to drop my figurative fisherman's net and do my part, whatever it might be, in his work?

While Jesus observed the Torah strictly during his lifetime and taught others to do so as well, he also commanded that his Gospel be taught to all nations. I couldn't do that by waiting. And it might not be possible to observe the Torah in a satisfactory Jewish way while, for example, serving a full-time mission. I didn't imagine that as a missionary, for example, I'd be able to go build a *sukkah*, a shelter of woven branches, during the week of the Sukkot holiday, or go without eating anything leavened during Passover. Going into people's homes simultaneously as a guest and as a representative of the Church of Jesus Christ of Latter-day Saints, I doubted it would be appropriate to ask if they cooked kosher. I knew enough to suspect that being a fully engaged Latter-day Saint would also involve departures from the way Rabbi Raphael had taught me to live the Torah.

I wasn't sure that Jesus or other figures in the scriptures had given permission for someone under the Jewish covenant to drop their original obligations. But some aspects of being a good disciple might mean I would have to live as a compromised Jew.

◇ ▢ ◇

I was on a choir trip to San Antonio, Texas that spring (the spring of my senior year) with Shea, Dave, and Matt when Shea gave me some unexpected news. His girlfriend had confided in him that my girlfriend was involved with someone else. I had known that she'd wondered about dating other people at some point: she'd told me she didn't want to break up but was nervous my future plans might take me out of Phoenix, where she wanted to stay. She'd mentioned that she wouldn't want an exclusive long-distance relationship. I didn't know she might already be moving on to someone else, though. She hadn't found a way to tell me yet, but she had already kissed him.

Looking back, I could tell myself it wasn't a big deal. That it was just a high school relationship. And in the long run, that's true. But it hit me so hard at the time. I really, really cared about her. And, if I'm honest, the way I thought about the relationship had gotten tied up with the way I saw myself. It wasn't by accident that my girlfriend was Jewish. Imagining a future with her had been a continuing anchor point connecting me to a Jewish life. My physical reaction to knowing I was losing her was inextricable from the pain of a severed tie to my people. That night, it all hit me at once. In the moment Shea broke the news, I could feel exactly what people meant by heartbreak. Crushing, sickening heartbreak.

"No, no, no. This can't be happening," I said. "What am I going to do?"

My three Mormon friends gathered around me. They couldn't answer my question, they didn't even try. They just said. "We're here for you. We're all here for you."

We all shared the same room for the trip. Boy, I sure needed those brothers.

I started to weep, violently. My world, all the delusions which had also been some of my dearest dreams, started to crumble. I felt like throwing up.

When it got late, I couldn't sleep. I didn't dare to try. My chest felt tight. My throat felt tight. I felt like I could barely breathe.

Matt Nelson was a little older than the rest of us. He was already eighteen, and he'd recently received the Melchizedek Priesthood in preparation for his mission. "Jason," he asked. "Would you like me to give you a priesthood blessing?"

"Yes," I said. "I really need that. What is it?"

Matt explained, then laid his hands gently on my head. Quietly, reverently, he began to bless me.

"Brother Jason Matthew Olson, by the authority of the Melchizedek Priesthood which I hold, I give you a blessing of comfort and peace during your time of heartbreak. I bless you to know that your Heavenly Father is totally aware of you at this time. He loves you so much and He has watched you, hoping you will make the decision to turn to Him in your time of suffering. I bless you to turn your heart to Him and give your life to His service. I bless you that you will be able to prepare for your baptism with faith, and miracles will come your way," said Matt.

I felt like a huge weight had been lifted from me. The pain was still there, but it was no longer crushing. No longer suffocating. "Thank you for that," I said. (I didn't mind that Matt presumed I would be baptized. After all, I had asked Shea to do just that two years earlier.)

"Will you all pray with me?" I asked the three of them.

"Of course, Jason," they said.

We prayed for my comfort and peace, my repentance, and my turning to God, never to look back.

That night taught me that salvation could come right along with suffering. That there may be anguish on the path God had given me, but that he would never leave me to walk it alone.

That night of heartbreak strengthened my relationship with God and my commitment to the gospel just in time. The end of my senior year was approaching. I was almost 18, old enough to be able to make my own decisions about baptism. Even though my mom still disapproved, I was ready to meet with the missionaries and prepare.

I had been studying the restored Gospel with Shea, Dave, and Matt for years, so I wasn't a typical "investigator." Still, I loved taking the lessons. Members of the ward opened up their houses to host the lessons. Spending time with the missionaries made me want even more to become one myself.

The missionaries seemed genuinely excited about the gospel and thrilled to work with someone who joyfully embraced it, even if some of my questions probably seemed very strange to them. We had a long talk once, for example, about the gender of the Holy Ghost. For them, that must have seemed like an odd fixation, but for me seeing the Holy Ghost as female was the easiest way to map the *Shechinah*, a feminine term for God's presence, from Judaism onto Mormon belief.

Probably because he was getting ready for his own mission, Matt had recently been called as a ward missionary. He went out regularly on "splits" with the missionaries, accompanying one or both of them to lessons with other people interested in the Book of Mormon or the message of the gospel's restoration or in joining the Church. As he worked with the missionaries, Matt had an idea. Why not bring me, an investigator, out on missionary appointments to testify to the other investigators about the truth of the gospel?

That sounded great to me. I went on splits, even though I wasn't a member yet. The missionaries, Matt, and I would go into an investigator's home, and I'd tell them my story. I'd tell them how much the Book of Mormon had meant to me, and shared my conviction that God spoke through that book. I talked about my appreciation for Joseph Smith and my gratitude for a modern prophet. It felt good just to share what I'd experienced and how I interpreted it. Call it what you will— Holy Ghost, Shechinah, spiritual electricity—but as we'd talk, I'd feel again that God was there.

That feeling was swirling in my chest, energizing me and pressing me forward. On one visit, I felt moved to say, "I have found that what these missionaries are teaching you is true. I've decided to be baptized. Will you come to my baptism?"

I didn't know how to reconcile the different parts of myself. I didn't know what the fallout in my family might be when my first adult decision was to embrace another religion. I just knew it felt right. And I trusted that feeling.

The missionaries were surprised, but happy, about my sudden announcement. Since I'd just invited people to come, they had a discussion with me about making baptism preparations. Some of those were spiritual: a kind of introspection and repentance like for Yom Kippur, but with the added weight of making a new covenant. Others were logistical: the missionaries wanted to set a date so they could schedule the baptismal font, set up my baptismal interview, and so on.

I put the spiritual preparation first. I told the missionaries I would go and make amends with anyone I had wronged and then we could set a date.

CHAPTER SIX

WASHED CLEAN

◇

I was serious about concrete acts of repentance. I thought through my relationships and who I should be apologizing to and asking forgiveness from. There was a member of the high school football team, for example, who I'd had a rocky relationship with. I could recognize my faults there and I worked to patch things up. It felt good to do that. Even though it would have been easy at graduation to move on with my life, it was satisfying to set something right.

Not all my relationships were getting better, though. My mom was getting panicked. Not only was I leaving the Jewish religious community, I was doing it by becoming a Mormon. My dad, though less involved in my religious life, wasn't happy either. He'd had a bad experience with some Latter-day Saints he'd done business with, and that had shaped his impression of the whole community. His mom and stepdad also had very negative things to say about Mormon theology and hoped to see my conversion stopped. They had a vivid mental image of what might happen to me, in this life and the next, if I went through with this.

It's interesting. My mother and I both bristled at any sign

of anti-Semitism, but as Jews we were in a position to know how misleading and wrongheaded anti-Semitic claims are. Because of that, we knew better than to listen to every criticism or to judge all of Judaism by the conduct of an individual Jew. My mother didn't have the same grounding though, when it came to anti-Mormon claims. She was genuinely concerned I was being brainwashed, that the organization I would be part of was actively dangerous. It pained her deeply to see me making the choice I was.

Had I wronged my mother? I didn't feel like I had in any sense that required repentance. Some of the pain we cause comes from sin; some just comes from the tensions of living. There is no easy answer for what to do when we want different things. The fact that we often see the world in starkly different ways makes it even harder to be comfortable with each other. I had kept my bargain to study with Rabbi Raphael—and my life had been deeply blessed as a result. But because that study had not convinced me to abandon my connection to Mormonism, my mother felt compelled to try other approaches.

The spring of my senior year, she booked plane tickets to Los Angeles. She'd found a group there called "Jews for Judaism," which shared Rabbi Singer's concern for protecting young Jews against Christian proselytizing. Their approach was different, however. While Rabbi Singer had focused on promoting Jewish interpretation of scriptures, "Jews for Judaism" went on the offensive. I spent an entire day with their lead rabbi, Rabbi Kravitz, discussing what he viewed as the problems of The Church of Jesus Christ of Latter-day Saints.

In some ways, it was something I'd longed for: a rabbi who knew something about the Book of Mormon. But because his goal was to discredit the faith rather than engage with me in a genuine religious dialogue about it, we turned out not to have a way to connect. It was like we were speaking different languages. My points of connection and his criticisms just didn't intersect.

For example, I remember him showing me a Latter-day Saint manual for converting Jewish people to the restored Gospel. He expected me to be offended that such a manual existed—that by knowing Latter-day Saints had targeted Jews for conversion, it would make them seem insincere, disrespectful, manipulative. In my own experience, however, Latter-day Saints had not come across as coercive. I also knew that they reached out to everyone, which made their missionary work feel less like a statement on Jewish insufficiency than a general outreach.

And I didn't need to see a manual to know that Latter-day Saints wanted to reach Jews. I still remembered how directly addressed I felt reading the title page of the Book of Mormon. My thought was, "If the Book of Mormon is true and was written for the House of Israel, why would Latter-day Saints not want to offer it to Jews?"

For me, the Book of Mormon belonged in conversation with the Hebrew Bible. Treating the Church as only a contemporary movement, without spiritual and philosophical weight, missed my mark. Rabbi Kravitz eventually realized that I was a sincere believer in the Book of Mormon and that I had studied it out for myself. He realized it would be impossible to dissuade me through only one conversation about a conclusion I had come to by faith.

It would have been totally understandable if that had been frustrating to him. If he had thrown up his hands and told my mother this was pointless, that I was too brainwashed to reach. But he didn't. Graciously, he began searching for common ground. Convinced that I would join another religious organization, Rabbi Kravitz began asking questions, searching to see what Jewish identity I still had left in me. If he couldn't talk me out of conversion, he wanted to shore up and preserve whatever Judaism he could in my life.

I love that impulse. I have seen it among so many people with a deep love for Judaism. Jewish memory has been passed down to the present only through heroic efforts and against incredible odds. It has meant so much for me to know that many people in the community have wanted to help me continue carrying that memory. Maybe Rabbi Kravitz was only trying to show me, a seventeen year old just about to begin his independent adult life, that the Jewish community had room for me if my commitment to Mormonism turned out to be only a phase. Part of what I felt in his questions, though, was a sense that Jewish spiritual identity went deeper than a decision about where and how to worship. That there was something inside me that still deserved to be tended, no matter where my life went.

I wasn't able to connect with Rabbi Kravitz in the way my mother wanted or that he had anticipated. I appreciated his willingness to meet me instead on a level I needed. I constantly felt torn, afraid of losing the Jewish part of my soul. His obvious desire to keep that Jewish part of me alive strengthened me. I wanted to keep it alive, too.

◇ ◻ ◇

Under the pressure of the moment, however, my family still wasn't ready to adapt their approach like Rabbi Kravitz had. From their point of view, the Jews for Judaism visit had been a failure. My testimony of the Book of Mormon was still intact. I still wanted to be baptized. In their struggle to come to terms with my decision, family members turned to another explanation: maybe my embracing Mormonism was a sign that I was mentally ill.

I later learned that my case was hardly unique. Religion is so woven into the rhythms of family life, into the assumptions we take for granted, that it often creates a crisis when a family member wants to join an unfamiliar group. People sometimes turn to any explanation, any social structure, in their attempts to prevent a jarring change. The historical record is full of examples of the first, pioneer generation of Latter-day

Saints going through the same types of resistance I did. Families often turned to clergy first. When that failed, they shifted to other sources of authority. In the 1800s, families sometimes labeled a person who wanted to convert as having *monomania*, or insanity confined to one subject.

In any case, my parents had me taken to two different psychologists.

The first counselor framed the situation in terms of the tension I was causing in my family. She couldn't see how my connection to a mere book could possibly be worth the anguish I was causing. Since she weighed the relative importance of spiritual conviction and immediate-term family harmony differently than I did, she couldn't see how my actions made sense. "You're not thinking straight," she said at one point of frustration.

Since she couldn't understand me, though, she couldn't reach me. Our sessions didn't get anywhere because she couldn't help me see a path forward that preserved both my family harmony and my sense of integrity. I told her I felt like I *was* thinking clearly. "You're acting like all the Latter-day Saints here in Arizona are delusional people," I said. "I can assure you that they're not. They're some of the most upstanding people I know."

My family decided to try a different counselor.

The second counselor took a more balanced approach. He was also Jewish, and could understand how difficult this might be for the family. But he didn't operate from a fixed assumption about my best religious course. He was concerned instead with understanding my subjective values and helping me construct a healthy mental model around them.

"Tell me why you want to become a Mormon," he asked me early. And then he listened.

I told him. About the Book of Mormon, my questions about the Messiah, my longing for a prophetic voice in the modern world, the compelling teachings I found in Mormonism. "I don't want to disappoint my family but I really do believe in the Book of Mormon," I said. I told him I felt like it was vitally important for me spiritually to join the Church.

"That sounds fine with me, from a psychological standpoint," he said. "You need to have integrity with yourself and live the life that is congruent with who you are and what you believe." Then he asked the hard question, the one I really wanted to talk with someone about. "How do you reconcile becoming a Mormon with your Jewish life and heritage?"

"That's the difficult part for me," I admitted. "I want to be Jewish, but I can't shake my belief in Jesus and the Book of Mormon." I thought about it. Despite my belief in Jesus, I doubted that my grandmother's Lutheran tradition would have been as compelling to me. I struggled with Martin Luther. For that matter, I preferred the Epistle of James, which Luther didn't care for, to much of what he found significant in Paul's writings. I certainly hadn't felt drawn to the crude evangelical attempts, inspired by ideas about Christ's name and grace, that had been made to convert me. When my friend's cousin had cornered me in a garage and told me I would go to hell unless I confessed that Jesus was my Lord, it had felt like an assault.

Though there were almost certainly spiritually abusive Mormons out there, the Mormonism I had come to know didn't feel at all like that. They had temples. They talked about covenants. They both taught and lived a sense of peoplehood, of collective relationship between God and a people. And their theology made explicit room for me. "I suppose what helps me is that the Book of Mormon was written for Jewish people and the House of Israel. The book honors Jewish people as the covenant people of God." While accepting Mormon ordinances would take me out of the mainstream of modern Jewish identity, I felt like there was a deeper compatibility with our past. "It doesn't ask me to abandon my Jewish heritage but honors it."

He nodded. Whatever he may have thought, personally, about Mormonism, he could see that in my life there was room to address, if not resolve, the tension between two identities. "What does your new faith teach you about your family?" he asked next.

This was a point that meant a lot to me. "It teaches that families are meant to be eternal," I said. And not just those of us living between the same four walls: Mormons believed in linking together chains of ancestors. The connection I felt to my grandparents and, through them, to my ancestors in eastern Europe, was sacred in Mormonism. "I do want to be with my family forever. Apparently, families can get sealed forever in the temples of the Church. I don't want to give up my family in any way. I want to be with them here on earth and in heaven."

He said, "Well amen to that, brother. That sounds great."

He had long since won my trust, so I pressed forward. "The problem, I think, is that that would require my family to join this Church," I admitted. "They're not interested in that." And then I realized something. "My hope that they'll not only support me but also maybe join me in conversion might be adding to the conflict in my family."

"I'm glad you have discovered that," he said. "How can I help you preserve your relationship with your family?"

There were no easy answers, but I had to hope we could all do our part. If they could accept the sincerity of my beliefs and I could find the right ways to show that I respected their position, we would make it through. I loved them. They loved me. Sometimes, though, it's that very love that makes us stumble, that makes us feel like we have to save each other.

◇ ▢ ◇

I turned 18 in June. With the missionaries, I'd set a baptismal date of August 16, 2003.

Faced with that looming deadline, my mother decided to make one more attempt to prevent me from making what she saw as a terrible mistake. She contacted a man named Rick Ross, who promoted himself as an anti-cult specialist who could "deprogram" cult members. I later learned that he had a track record of using ethically controversial techniques, which had landed him in legal trouble.

Rick Ross flew out from New Jersey and to our home on a contract to deprogram me. His approach was aggressive. Like human beings were a wolf pack and he was trying to establish dominance. For three days, he used a combination of attacks, pulling document after document from a file to build his case that Joseph Smith was a fraud and the Church of Jesus Christ of Latter-day Saints was a destructive cult. It didn't feel like a reasoned case, though, as much as a hazing. The ceaseless barrage of accusations and insinuations felt a lot more like brainwashing to me than anything I'd experienced with the Latter-day Saints.

I didn't respect his tactics because they weren't respectful of me. He relied on a long tradition of literature attacking Joseph Smith and the Book of Mormon, but what it really proved to me is that there was a long tradition of people attacking Joseph Smith and the Book of Mormon. Why should the shrillest critics command my attention when I had a broader context?

I finally asked Rick point blank if he had ever read the Book of Mormon.

"No, I haven't," he said. "But I've researched the Book of Mormon."

I said, "Rick, I've read the entire Book of Mormon and I know that it's scripture. I can't prove that, but that's faith."

I missed Rabbi Raphael. I missed Rabbi Kravitz. They didn't act like my beliefs were a totally secular question, like Rick Ross did, or that my embrace of Mormonism had to do with some mental failing on my part. They knew they weren't experts in Mormonism. Instead, they focused on showing me truth and beauty in the Torah and Judaism.

I had no doubt other people would be able to criticize both the Torah and Judaism, too. It would be really easy to assemble three days' worth of documents with ugly accusations: personal attacks on Jewish leaders, diatribes against our scripture, questions about whether we belonged in the same category as other religious groups. That wasn't just a thought experiment: ugly assaults on Jewish dignity were a recurring pattern in history. Some, like blood libels (rumors that Jews killed Christian children and used their blood to make matzah) or *The Protocols of the Elders of Zion* (a fake 1919 expose purporting to reveal Jewish plans for world domination) are blatantly false. Like attacks on any minority groups, others selectively mixed real textual passages or incidents with their readers' preconceived notions.

For every accusation against Mormonism, then, I would always wonder if it was the whole story. If it wasn't inaccurate or taken out of context. It is hard to establish truth by elimination, because nothing is left standing. Beauty isn't like that. If I had seen the spiritual beauty in a thing, whether it was the Torah or the Book of Mormon, you couldn't make a file thick enough to take away those moments. My mental models about an issue might change over time, but I would hold on to the core experience I'd been given.

Rick didn't deprogram me. He didn't convince me to cancel the date for my baptism. But he did teach me one vital lesson: that I could relate far better to a sincere believer of another faith than to someone from my own traditions, Jewish or Mormon, who didn't care about the beauty of the sacred. I have little patience for debunking any religion, whether in the service of your own faith or for reasons outside faith. In the end, what Rick gave me was a growing commitment to religious pluralism. A resolve to make room to see the good another person experienced within their own convictions.

After the exhaustion of three days with Rick Ross, I was afraid of whatever might come next. I'd made it through the challenges orchestrated by my immediate family. I'd waded through opposition from Jewish friends. I'd listened to my dad's stepfather, a Christian, tell me about how I must be under some Satanic influence to sign up for a surefire Mormon ticket to hell. If Satan was involved, though, I was pretty sure he didn't want me to get baptized and was the one throwing all these emotionally draining obstacles in my way. While the Rick Ross visit felt like my family's last-ditch effort to prevent my conversion, I was pretty sure that, theologically speaking, Satan was still all in.

I was 18 already. I could make my own choices. So two weeks before my baptism, I decided not to ask my parent's permission for a road trip. I left the house over my mom's objections and got on a bus to Utah. Slumped down in the seat as the Greyhound pulled out of Phoenix, I got out my cell phone and called Dave to ask if I could crash his family vacation there. I really hoped the answer would be yes.

"Hey buddy," I asked him, trying to sound casual. "What are you doing?"

"Just hanging at my Uncle's house in Provo."

"Well, guess what? I'm on my way to Provo right now by bus," I said, as if that were a totally normal thing for me to be doing.

"No way!" Dave said. "Can't wait till you get here. I'll show you around!"

It was so good to get off the bus and be able to coast a while on Dave's support. Jesus said in the gospels that if you follow him, you'll find brothers and sisters and mothers and fathers (Matt. 12:46–50). They were there for me when I needed them. So many times when I needed them.

From Provo, we followed the route of Utah's Jordan River up to Salt Lake City, built on the shores of a lake that had reminded Mormon settlers of the Dead Sea. I saw the Salt Lake Temple, with its "Holiness to the Lord" inscription, and the nearby Tabernacle, named after the worship space that sustained the children of Israel as they travelled through the wilderness. We went by the Assembly Hall, where I caught sight of the Stars of David that nineteenth century pioneer builders included over the doors.[1]

---

1. The Assembly Hall was completed in 1880, which Latter-day Saints

Here was another thing that a person like Rick Ross couldn't take away from me. He could call the Book of Mormon into question on historical grounds. He could've done the same for the Jewish exodus from Egypt, for which we have no real physical evidence. The nineteenth century Mormon migration, however, was undeniably real. Tens of thousands of Latter-day Saints had walked out past the edge of the settled eastern United States to seek refuge from persecution in a desert home. The physical signs of that exodus, the echoes of a sacred history, surrounded me. They haunted me. The land felt weighted with the intensity of its spiritual past; the air hung heavy with a longing for God.

I stayed with Dave's family for the rest of their vacation, drove back with them from Provo, and stayed with them the night before my baptism.

◇ ▢ ◇

I woke up the morning of my baptism feeling a lot of things. The strongest was excitement. I'd been preparing for this day for years and could hardly believe that now, after all the obstacles and lessons I'd made my way through, it had finally come.

I also felt some relief. It hadn't been easy getting here, and the strain on my family had been a heavy burden for all of us to bear. Now that I was getting baptized, it felt like the worst might be over and that, with time and mutual acceptance, things would improve. I had reason to hope. Shortly before my baptism, my grandfather had reached out to me. After listening to my feelings in a multi-day conversation, he said, "Jason, I can tell you sincerely believe in the Book of Mormon and Jesus. You know what? If you lived in the time of Jesus,

---

marked as a jubilee year (50 years since the Church's 1830 founding). The stars were included as a reference to the Biblical children of Israel, from whom the Saints were then borrowing practices like jubilee debt forgiveness.

I think you probably would have been one of his first disciples. . . . Now, I don't believe in any of that, but I respect that you do." I was moved to know that his relationship with me was more important than our differences. I wanted to live up to his example.

Finally, beneath the excitement and relief, there was an undeniable layer of mourning. The day of my baptism was a day when I said goodbye to the Jewish life I had imagined for myself. To the image of marrying traditionally, under a chuppah. To the idea of seeing my infant sons, if I had any, receive *brit milah* (circumcision). The white clothing I would be baptized in felt at once like a sign of purity and rebirth and like a burial shroud.

I got ready and went to the church with Dave's family for the Saturday baptismal service. To my surprise, there were probably 150 people who attended. Many were people I didn't even know, who had come not only from Shea's ward, but from other wards in the area. Latter-day Saints were showing their support and welcome for me.

No one from my family attended the baptism. It wasn't a joyful occasion for them, so it wasn't a surprise that they didn't come. The only Jewish person to attend, in fact, was my ex-girlfriend.

It meant a lot to me that she was there. We'd been good to each other and we'd hurt each other. It felt good to have her there on a day so focused on receiving and extending forgiveness. As we stumble our way through life, all of us are more than any moment or choice. I hope that in the next life, we'll honor the best in each other. The present is always a good time to start.

And it felt important to have one Jewish person there. One friend, one of my closest friends, to wish me well at this time of radical transition.

"Thank you for coming," I told her. "This means so much to me."

"Jason," she replied, "I just want you to be happy. I just

hope this will make you happy."

There wasn't a lot to the service. An opening prayer, a song, a short talk. Then Shea took me into the font. The water was warm! He showed me how to hold his arm and plug my nose, while he would fully immerse me. It was all familiar to him, even though I was the first person he ever baptized.

In the Book of Mormon, I'd read Nephi's promise about the step I was taking:

> Wherefore, my beloved brethren, I know that if ye shall follow the Son, with full purpose of heart, acting no hypocrisy and no deception before God, but with real intent, repenting of your sins, witnessing unto the Father that ye are willing to take upon you the name of Christ, by baptism—yea, by following your Lord and your Savior down into the water, according to his word, behold, then shall ye receive the Holy Ghost; yea, then cometh the baptism of fire and of the Holy Ghost; and then can ye speak with the tongue of angels, and shout praises unto the Holy One of Israel (2 Nephi 31:13).

Shea said my full name, as Latter-day Saints do when giving blessings, and spoke the simple baptismal prayer. I went down into the water, following my Savior into his death and burial, and came back up, following him into his resurrection. I put my sins to death in that watery grave and washed them clean in his name. I came out of the water feeling truly forgiven and pure. I was born again.

The next day, I went to Church. Before the sacrament, the ward's bishop laid his hands on my head and confirmed me a member of the Church of Jesus Christ of Latter-day Saints. "Receive the Holy Ghost," he told me. Part blessing, part command.

And I felt it. It was soft and still, but the baptism of fire entered my soul. I felt like I could sing now in some unseen choir, sing Hallelujah to God and his angels.

I had started a new life.

PART TWO

MAN ON A MISSION

CHAPTER SEVEN

FAMILIES CAN BE TOGETHER FOREVER

◇

After my baptism and confirmation, I went back home. It was awkward. I had literally run away for a trip to Utah and come back to Arizona just in time to join the Church of Jesus Christ of Latter-day Saints. They were understandably frustrated and disappointed. They were also scared sick I would go on a mission for the Church next and the two years spent on service would derail and ultimately ruin my life.

I could have stayed longer with Dave or Shea. However awkward our time together might be, though, I was just two weeks away from starting my freshman year of college at the University of Arizona, so I wanted to spend time with my parents. They loved me and I loved them. Conversion doesn't change that, even if it complicates it. Just being around each other was an important reassurance for all of us. When the time came, my dad volunteered to drive me from our home in Scottsdale down to drop me off at the U of A campus in Tucson. We didn't talk about my conversion at all on the car ride. The important thing was just to be around each other.

To have the reassurance that we still knew how to share space and time.

It was hard not to feel a little isolated in this new chapter of my life, though, as my dad pulled away. I didn't know a single Latter-day Saint in Tucson. All my Mormon friends from Scottsdale had decided to go to Brigham Young University or were already on missions. I knew some people on campus: a lot of my high school friends were living there. I just wasn't sure how much support they'd be in helping me avoid or resist the temptations of campus life.

I hadn't been on campus long when I went to hang out with old friends at a frat house where the school's Jewish fraternity threw parties. Some of the people there were good high school friends. Confused as they were about my conversion, they were still happy to make space for me. Several of them wanted me to pledge.

As it happened, though, I was there on a night when they'd invited a local stripper to perform. That wasn't an unusual thing for college students to do, but it drove home how I'd really gone through two conversions: both to a different faith and to a deeper level of religiosity. Faith gave me the strength to stand out, as steady as Shea with the pornographic magazine when we were in junior high. As steady as many observant Jews would have been in preserving their own convictions about appropriate sexuality. Once I realized what was about to happen, I left. I never went back. I'd still hang out with those friends at their apartments or restaurants, but didn't feel comfortable going back to the frat house as a shared social space. That kind of brotherhood, of fraternity, was not for me.

I was desperate for a refuge. Fortunately, Latter-day Saints understand that problem and have been working for generations to address it on campuses. I became very active in the campus Latter-day Saint Institute of Religion. At Institute, I took religion classes, attended dances and recreational activities, and got involved in group service projects they organized.

Through the Institute, I was also able to join a local Latter-day Saint traveling choir called *Millennium*. Just like in high school, my singing life became an anchoring part of my social life. The choir's president, Michael Orr, became a great friend and mentor.

In my freshman year of college, as I was getting my bearings in Latter-day Saint life away from the first Church friend group I'd known, I was also trying to sort out what I could still do to stay connected in some way with Jewish life. Though roommates were assigned randomly, I'd been lucky enough to get a Jewish roommate. As he talked about life and plans, one thing that came up was that he was looking forward to taking a ten-day trip to Israel supported by the Birthright Israel Foundation. Ever since my bar mitzvah, I'd been excited to visit the land of Israel on a Birthright trip of my own.

Well, if the trip was really based on a birthright, nothing had changed about how I was born. My religious conversion hadn't changed who my mother was, hadn't changed my ancestral connection to dream of a return to Israel. Longing for a continued connection to my people and history, I decided to apply.

The application, though, asked for my religion. I noted that I was a Latter-day Saint. Then I met with the Birthright director assigned to campus to explain my situation.

"I was raised Jewish and my mother is Jewish," I said. "I really want to go on this trip. I won't proselytize in any way," I added. As much as I loved missionary work, I recognized that there are appropriate and inappropriate contexts for sharing beliefs, and that a trip designed to foster Jewish identity needed to be focused on Jewish identity. "I just want to connect with my Jewish roots."

She was sympathetic, but the eligibility regulations were clear. "I'm sorry, Jason," she said. "But because you converted to the Latter-day Saints, you are no longer eligible to go on the Birthright trip."

That was hard for me. Israel was more for me than a passing desire: I felt a spiritual thirst to connect with the land. The Birthright trip wasn't my only option for going. But the confirmation that I'd lost my eligibility still hit home. Had I, like Esau in Genesis, sold my birthright?

I pushed aside thoughts of going to Israel in the most Latter-day Saint way possible. My nineteenth birthday was that summer: I could go straight on a mission instead. I found out what preparation was needed and started down the list. Got the wisdom teeth taken out, did the physical, the whole shebang. Alongside the physical preparation, there were also overtly religious things to do by way of preparation.

One of these was to receive my patriarchal blessing. This involved an old man, a sort of Mormon *tzaddik*, laying his hands on my head and, after the model of Biblical patriarchs blessing their children, giving me a blessing with promises about my life. During such blessings, a patriarch also declares a lineage for each church member in one of the tribes of Israel. Most are told in their blessings that they belong to the tribes of Ephraim or Manasseh, tasked in Latter-day Saint thought with missionary work and the modern gathering of Israel. I was told instead that I was part of the tribe of Judah. Within Latter-day Saint understanding, then, Jewish heritage remained an important part of my identity and spiritual life.

The last step felt like the most significant: getting ready to go to the temple for my endowment ceremony. I prepared diligently to attend the temple but had no idea what to expect. The word "endowment" was taken from the New Testament. At the end of the Gospel of Luke, Jesus told his disciples to wait in Jerusalem until they were endowed with power from on high (Luke 24:49). The gospel says "they returned to Jerusalem with great joy, and were continually in the temple, praising and blessing God" (Luke 24:52–53).

I knew that at least some of the imagery in the temple came from the Hebrew Bible. I'd been to the temple fonts, held up on the backs of twelve carved oxen like the "molten sea" in Solomon's temple, as described in 1 Kings 7. I knew there were other parallels: a succession of courts, a veil in the temple, and so on. But because the temple experience is supposed to be individually experienced and interpreted, there's not much direct Latter-day Saint commentary on what exactly the temple endowment will be like. People tend to talk around it; they refer to temple ordinances in generalities, leaving the details for each person to experience fresh.

While keeping within that tradition, I will say that I wasn't prepared for how the experience hit me. In the Book of Exodus, after Moses receives the Ten Commandments, there are chapters and chapters of instruction on how the Israelites' wilderness tabernacle should be built and what the priests do there. The ritual clothing, the washing and anointing, and a lot of the physical set up of the space is clearly designed to collapse time and help link each person back to that ancient mode of worship.

The themes of the temple also spoke specifically to my Jewish longings. The language of covenant, the awareness that I was receiving the promises of Abraham, Isaac, and Jacob, moved and strengthened me. I felt I had truly partaken of the restoration of my temple and my blessings. I was endowed with power from on high to accomplish my mission.

As I reflected on my temple experience, I thought of the Latter-day Saint teaching that there was a great apostasy, a fundamental drift sometime in Christian history from the balance of truth Jesus taught. Christians believe that first century Jews missed something by not accepting Jesus. But from a Latter-day Saint perspective, it seems clear that Christians missed something by rejecting the significance of the temple. Jews, even without a physical temple, continued to honor the temple's memory in their worship, prayers, and calendar. In my view, both groups, while preserving the things that mattered most to them, missed something vital and threw off the balance of the whole.

Many Protestant critics of Mormonism believe the Church of Jesus Christ went "beyond" a restoration of the New Testament church. Latter-day Saints' use of imagery and themes from the "Old" Testament can be particular areas of concern. In some Protestant perspectives, our restored gospel is like an overgrown garden badly in need of aggressive trimming. For me, though, the many elements of Mormonism that go beyond a stripped-down primitive Church based only on the New Testament were exactly what made the faith so compelling.

To me, it's clear that the Church has gone beyond basic Christian primitivism. Because Moses, Elias, and Elijah brought Old Testament Priesthood keys to the Prophet Joseph Smith in 1836, at the Kirtland Temple, the restored Church has a very Hebraic feel. The living prophet has keys both to gather Israel and bestow blessings of the Abrahamic covenant on couples sealed in the temple, as well as authority to perform all the ordinances of the temple for the dead (see Doctrine & Covenants 110). As a Jew, I thought it was great that Old Testament prophets were part of the Restoration of the Church—and I still believe they had a profound effect on how the process unfolded.

Not long after I attended the temple, the day came when I received my mission call. On the forms I filled out, I'd instructed Church headquarters to mail it directly to Shea Owens' home in Scottsdale. (That felt like the kindest way for the news to come.)

I was thrilled to pick up the envelope, eager to find out where God wanted me to go. Feeling it in my hands made the dream feel so real. I was really going to be a missionary, really going to share the restored gospel I had come to love so deeply with people somewhere in the world. I tore the envelope open. The letter, which bore the signature of President Gordon B. Hinckley, called me to serve in the New Jersey Morristown Mission, which also includes parts of New York state. I immediately recognized it as a place with one of the highest concentrations of Jews in the US. Being called to this area felt like a message that God knew me. Somehow this experience might help me clarify my wrestlings with my Jewish heritage and Latter-day Saint faith.

I knew it would be hard on my parents for me to serve. I'd be gone for two years. I'd be dropping out of college, and they had no guarantee I'd go back. I'd imagine that sending sons out on missions isn't easy even for families who go back generations in the Church. For my family, though, like for those of many converts, my call meant going through all those hardships and a double dose of uncertainty—all for something they had not asked for, and which would be a source of shame rather than honor for anyone who asked in my absence how Jason was doing.

I knew they were worried about how a mission might change me. Worried about what our relationship might be like while I was gone and when I came back. I didn't want them to hurt, but I didn't know what to do about it. Though I worried it might feel like salt on their wounds, I turned to a Latter-day Saint song, "Families Can Be Together Forever," to express my love for them before I left.

Tears ran down my face as I sang. "I want to be a part of this family, forever," I told them.

And then, in what must have seemed like a terrible irony to them and felt like a kind of paradox even to me, I left them.

CHAPTER EIGHT

UNTO ALL NATIONS. . . IN NEW JERSEY

◇

A Mormon mission is a wonderful, difficult experience. It focuses your attention inward at the same time as it pushes you out into the world. It's a spiritual experience that also raises the tension level on all your unresolved religious questions. It's a time that can be isolating and lonely while also giving you an abundance of new and unexpected relationships.

As a missionary, I spent more time with other Latter-day Saints than I ever had before. During my brief stay in the Missionary Training Center, everyone I saw was a member of my new faith. In New Jersey, I always had another missionary as an assigned companion to study scriptures with and to work alongside.

During the day, though, we would go out and talk with anyone who would take time for us within our large assigned areas. At home in Arizona, I spent almost all my time in the same few places where I always studied and socialized. Missionary service

is a completely different way to get to know a place: we went everywhere. We missionaries came to know and love people from
all kinds of backgrounds, in all kinds of neighborhoods, dealing
with all kinds of things.

New Jersey attracted immigrants from around the world,
so the first part of my mission gave me a very multicultural experience. For example, I quickly grew close to two Nepali investigators, Maya and Shiva. After growing up Hindu, both—like
me—had felt drawn to Jesus. They were still searching, though,
for the right church to join.

There's a story the Jewish mystic Isaac ben Luria told: that
in the beginning of the world, God sent vessels filled with divine light toward the world, but the vessels cracked and scattered the light everywhere. For some Jews, this explains why
Israel was scattered from its homeland into exile. That exile,
called *galut* in Hebrew, is tied up with associations of pain and
alienation, but Luria's story suggested it was also purposeful.
By being scattered, Jews were in a position to find lost light.

As a Mormon missionary, my commission was likewise to
gather. Latter-day Saints believe that there are pieces of God's
truth and goodness everywhere. Our purpose, then, is not to
attack people's spiritual foundations, but to build on them.
"You bring with you all the good that you have, and let us add
to it," Gordon B. Hinckley said while he was our prophet.[1] I had
brought so much from Judaism. Maya and Shiva could bring
the best of their own Hindu upbringings as they built their
own understanding of the restored gospel. Together, we could
create a shared community more beautiful than anything we
could have imagined alone.

The Church of Jesus Christ of Latter-day Saints is at its
best when it is a link between old traditions and new insights,
rather than as a total replacement for what people had before.

---

1. "Words of a Living Prophet," *Liahona*, June 1997, churchofjesuschrist.
org

I didn't have a lot of experience with the traditions Maya and Shiva came from, but was happy to learn a little as I taught. I had also never eaten Nepali food before, but fell in love with it as they fed us and we shared our message and community with them. They went through the missionary lessons quickly, attended Church with us every Sunday, and decided to be baptized. I was able to walk down into the font with them, just like Shea had done for me, and share that moment with my two dear friends.

In Jersey City, I got to know Farooq. He was already a member of the Church, but another model of how to integrate two identities. He'd been raised Muslim and worked as a real estate broker in Egypt. He was well-off and well-respected when he felt drawn to Christianity and was caught worshipping at a Coptic church in Cairo. In Egypt, departure from Islam was counted as a betrayal of the Muslim community: Farooq paid a high social price for conscience. Living as much an exile as an immigrant in the United States, he reached out to missionaries to continue his spiritual journey. Like me, the Book of Mormon played a central role in his conversion and, like me, he loved to come out with missionaries on visits, especially among Arabic-speakers.

I still remember Farooq's reaction when he found out I was a Jew. "I love the Jews!" he said. "We are cousins!" While conflict over the state of Israel has dominated the public image of Jewish-Arab relations, it is not the only reality. Our cultures have crossed paths over the centuries and left their mark on each other, whether in Moorish Spain or the Ottoman Empire. In the distant past, Jews and Arabs claim a shared ancestry from Abraham. No matter what issues we may face in the present, that shared heritage can also give us moments of closeness and connection. And in Mormon belief, that familial connection, however distant, matters deeply.

The Latter-day Saint belief that families can be sealed together for eternity extends to our ancestors. "For we without them cannot be made perfect; neither can they without us be made perfect," our scriptures say (see Doctrine & Covenants 128:18). The temple work Latter-day Saints do for the dead is meant to offer everyone who ever lived the chance to be linked together in chains of relationships across time and space. In our newfound faith, Farooq and I really did share the bonds of a great family in need of reconciliation and reconnection.

My mission gave me new chances to connect with my family's eastern European roots as well. Laura and Detre were investigators from Hungary. While their food was different than anything I had tasted, a few of the things they made shared just enough culinary DNA with my grandmother's Ashkenazi cooking to bring back treasured memories.

Laura and Detre weren't attending religious services much by the time we met them, but had never given up on God. They had so many questions, deep questions, about the restored gospel. They were like the wise child in the Passover seder. There's a temptation for people in positions of religious authority, even an authority as simple as that of a young missionary, to give in to their own insecurity and resent or resist questions. But questions are at the heart of the best teaching. A revelation in the Doctrine and Covenants, given through Joseph Smith, describes true gospel teaching like this: "Wherefore, he that preacheth and he that receiveth, understand one another, and both are edified and rejoice together" (Doctrine & Covenants 50: 22). It was a thrill to teach people with sincere questions that stretched us.

My companion at the time was Rafael Drotar. He was an immigrant from eastern Europe, too: born and raised in Romania. He'd been a faithful member of a Romanian Pentecostal Church when he became interested in Mormonism. He and I wanted to give everyone we taught the same serious spiritual attention we had craved. Raf and I often dedicated our morning companionship study to searching for things to show Laura and Detre in response to their questions. We had to research, study, ponder, and pray to find the right scriptural passage or insight to share. I'm grateful for the ways they pushed me: when we found something for them, it was also like a flood of truth for us. We were edified with them, and we all rejoiced together.

Another investigator I related to personally was Ikeji. He was from Nigeria. He was still a faithful Catholic when we met him, but was searching for something more. Almost immediately, he felt like a brother to us. He accepted our message but found overwhelming opposition from his family. I remember him breaking down in tears. I could relate so strongly. The tension between what you believe and what loved ones expect is a terrible burden.

I couldn't fix it for him. I couldn't tell him how things would turn out. So my companion and I offered what we could: a blessing. A priesthood blessing, like I'd been given on the night of heartbreak in high school when my breath felt tight.

Ikeji hadn't heard about or seen a priesthood blessing before, so we told him how, if he wanted, we could lay our hands on his head, bless him by the authority of the Melchizedek Priesthood, and offer words of comfort or counsel under the inspiration of the Holy Ghost.

"Please," he said. "I need this."

"Great," we told him. "Let's pull up this chair and you can sit here while we lay our hands on your head."

"No. Absolutely not," Ikeji replied. "I will kneel for the men of God."

In his reverence, I learned greater faith.

Around the same time I was worrying over Ikeji's tension with his family, we visited the Nolans. They were sincere, devout Catholics with no interest at the time in conversion. They wanted us to come, though, because their son had joined the Church of Jesus Christ of Latter-day Saints and was serving his own mission in Mongolia. They accepted his decision. They wanted to feed us, care for us, as a way of showing their love for him. It especially moved them to know that I was a convert. They felt like that connected him and me, across the distance, in some deeper, unseen way. One night, before my companion and I had to go, they expressed their feelings about how my presence helped them appreciate what their son was doing. Hearing the emotion in their voices, sensing their support for a son who left the path they'd expected him to follow, I broke down into tears. I couldn't seem to stop myself, so I let the tears shake me. I sobbed for what felt like an hour. How I envied the power in that love.

One family stands out in my memory. While I was serving in the suburbs of Somerset County, I met Jeff and Sharon and their children. Sharon had a Latter-day Saint coworker named Jono, and they'd become good friends. In 2004, the Church finished building a temple near Lincoln Center in Manhattan. Like the Temple in ancient Jerusalem, access to the inside of a Latter-day Saint temple is normally limited to those in the faith who have prepared themselves to enter. But between the time a temple is built and when it is dedicated, there's no religious restriction and anyone can take a tour of the temple interior to see what the buildings are like and hear about what happens inside after it is dedicated.

I believed, intellectually, that the temple was a big part of what historical Christianity had lost when Judaism and Christianity parted ways in the centuries after Jesus' ministry and death. Walking through the temple, Jeff and Sharon felt the Spirit of God. They felt like they had found something they'd been missing.

For many Christians, it's usually not a big deal to look for and find a new church. Becoming a Latter-day Saint, though, involves more than just switching a building or branding. It really is like a new religion. That may be why many insist that Latter-day Saints aren't Christian. On its surface, it's preposterous to argue that the Church *of Jesus Christ* of Latter-day Saints is not a Christian church. But for some people, it's hard to understand that there could be a whole different way of thinking about Christianity, that there could be another Christian religion so clearly distinct from their own.

By the time I met them, Jeff and Sharon were not yet baptized, but already involved in the life of the ward. Jeff even had a calling! I was proud of the bishop for having extended an appropriate assignment, creating a space for this good man to serve in the community, without waiting until he decided to commit his life to the faith first.

We taught Jeff and Sharon while I was there, but also spent hours on their back deck, talking about life and family. They became family to me. Sharon was like a second mom while I was away from home and she treated me like a second son. I still feel close to her and keep in touch with the family.

As New Jerseyians, Sharon and Jeff had good Jewish friends and appreciated Jewish culture. In addition to sharing her family's own favorite foods with me, she sometimes made me her special "Passover brisket." It reminded me of home.

In Sunday worship, we break bread and drink water together as the sacrament. That ritual has its roots in a basic, human truth. There's something sacred about just eating, talking, praying with other people. Something sacred in sharing worries, hopes, ideas, and dreams. Something sacred in taking time to weave lives together.

Jeff got ready for baptism while I was there as a missionary. Sharon needed more time and we didn't push her. We respected her, and so we respected her own spiritual timing. As it turned out, she decided to be baptized not too long after. And I still remember when she called me on the phone, after I was home from my mission and back in college, to say she and Jeff had gone back to the Manhattan temple—this time to be sealed together for time and eternity.

She'd also received her patriarchal blessing, a special once-in-a-lifetime blessing with words of counsel and prophecy, given by an older man specially set apart to act in a role like

Jacob at the end of Genesis or another of the Biblical patriarchs. A patriarch embodies the kind of manhood I most aspire to: a willingness to quietly bless and serve, offering people individual attention and insight. As part of the blessing, the patriarch declares a heritage for each Church member in a specific one of the Biblical twelve tribes of Israel. That confirmation of belonging not just to a church, but to a people, meant a lot to Sharon. "I am in the House of Israel," she told me, "just like you."

◇ ◻ ◇

The boundaries of my mission included Rockland County, New York. New York City, where about one in eight people are Jewish, has a much larger total Jewish population, but Rockland County, where about one in three people are Jewish, has the country's highest concentration of Jews. By the time I was there in the early 2000s, Rockland County's Jewish population was also disproportionately Orthodox compared to American Jews in general. Nationally, among Jews who belong to a synagogue, about one in ten are Orthodox while the majority are from the Reform or Conservative traditions.[2] As a further distinction, many of the Jews in Rockland County did not belong to the same modern Orthodox tradition as Rabbi Singer and Rabbi Rafael. Instead, they were *haredim* (meaning those who "tremble" before the word of God), a subset of Jews who reject modern secular culture in their search for piety.

Reform and Conservative Jews are largely able to blend into American society. People may notice we're Jewish because of things we've said, holidays we take off, or for some of us, by recognizing a typically Jewish surname. We may have some physical features that we think of as Jewish, but strangers on the street can't really pick out a Jewish face: Jews may look European, Middle Eastern, or African, depending on where in the

---

2. Pew Forum, "Jewish Americans in 2020," May 11, 2021, pewforum.org

global Jewish diaspora our ancestors settled.

Modern Orthodox Jewish men may be recognizable by the kippot they wear to cover their heads, in an echo of God's instruction to Moses to cover his head in God's presence. Modern Orthodox Jewish women dress modestly, but not necessarily in a way people would recognize. Because of traditions about clothing and hair, haredim are more recognizable. In Rockland County, you can tell there's a high Jewish population at a glance. They are willing to attract that attention. Since haredi communities tend to have close internal relationship ties and fewer strong ties outside of their communities, they're also more vulnerable to prejudice.

Having spent time studying with the modern Orthodox in Phoenix, sharing their space and admiring their books, I didn't have a problem spending time living in the midst of several Orthodox communities in New York. But it did raise questions for me.

For Mormons, the notion of covenant is vitally important. Everyone I met on my mission, whatever their religious and cultural background, had access to pieces of God's truth and built their lives around portions of his goodness. We wanted to offer them more, of course, but our goal wasn't just to sprinkle Mormon insights into people's lives. We also offered a chance to make covenants. When we talked about a restored gospel, or a restoration of Jesus Christ's church, we meant that a covenant had been restored, along with a restoration of priesthood authority for the ordinances associated with it.

At the same time, though, the Book of Mormon thoroughly resisted the common Christian idea that Jesus Christ's ministry had marked the end of God's covenant with the Jews. Again and again, the Book of Mormon insisted that God remembered his covenants. For example, the passage in 2 Nephi 29 that had caught my attention when I first read the Book of Mormon rebukes people who persecute Jews and concludes with a reminder of covenant. "I will show unto them that fight against my word and against my people, who are of the house of Israel," the scripture says, "that I am God, and that I covenanted with Abraham that I would remember his seed forever." The Doctrine & Covenants expands on the idea. A passage on priesthood, for example, explains that the descendants of Aaron, or *kohenim*, still carry a lineal priesthood (68: 18–19). The restored covenants in the Church existed alongside, rather than replacing, God's other covenants. Cumorah, where Joseph Smith had been given the plates with the Book of Mormon record, supplemented rather than supplanted Sinai.

Within a Latter-day Saint understanding, then, baptism was not my first covenant. I already belonged to a covenant God made with Israel. So did the Jews I'd see each day on the streets of Rockland County. That was true of the Reform, Conservative, modern Orthodox, and secular Jews I might pass without noticing.When they worked toward the goal of *tikkum olam*, or repairing the world through acts of goodness, they were doing God's work as surely as I was. And whether they lit candles on the Sabbath, kept holidays, or tended their connection to the Jewish past through literature and museums, these people were keeping alive a tradition that I believe had divine significance. Seeing the haredim, though, made it especially obvious. Surrounded by these examples of conspicuous Jewish faith, I could feel Sinai tugging at me. Everywhere I turned in Rockland County, I could see signs of the covenant. I could feel it; I could almost taste it.

Honestly, that made me feel a little guilty. Rabbi Raphael had emphasized that as a Jew, it was my duty to live the Torah whether Jesus was the Messiah or not. For practical reasons, I'd bent on my understanding of that obligation. As a representative of the Church of Jesus Christ of Latter-day Saints, for example, I didn't think it would be fair to the Nepali or Hungarian or Nigerian or American-born people I taught to worry about whether their food was kosher. I didn't want to confuse them about what the Church taught or needlessly complicate their hospitality. The more pressing value for me at that time was to reach out and remove barriers of understanding between the people I met and the restored gospel.

But even if I was justified in those choices about observance, even if Cumorah really did need to take precedence over Sinai in some of my decisions, what did I have to offer to Jewish people who were more conscientious than I was in honoring our ancestral covenant? For me, it was a serious theological question.

CHAPTER NINE

ROCKLAND COUNTY

◇

When I was a teenager listening to Rabbi Tovia Singer, I had wanted to be a great Jewish counter-missionary to keep Jews strong in their Judaism and resist Christianity. Instead, just six years later, I found myself as a Latter-day Saint missionary in the most Jewish county in the United States, trying to figure out where I fit and what God wanted me to do.

In a strange twist of fate, I ended up looking for answers about how my own Latter-day Saint convictions related to my Jewish identity among the Messianic Jews Rabbi Singer and others had warned me against in my teens. I had heard about their community before, but what did I really know about it? When I became a Latter-day Saint, I'd wished people would take time to understand the tradition on its own terms, and not only from hearsay or through the lens of antagonists. After talking it through with my companion, we decided to attend Shabbat services (held Friday and Saturday, in keeping with Jewish tradition) at Messianic synagogues to get to know the community ourselves.

What I found there was not intentional deception but sincere belief. There were wonderful people there, who shared my interest in how to reconcile their belief in Jesus as the Messiah with the anchoring presence of Jewish traditions. We had both stepped out of the broad and diverse space occupied by normative Judaism in its various branches. We'd taken markedly different paths, however, and come to different conclusions about what our faiths meant.[1]

The first and most obvious difference between us was that Messianic Jews claimed to be "completed Jews," more fully Jewish because of their belief in Jesus. I saw myself instead as a compromised Jew. For me, Mormonism and Judaism showed me the same God from different angles. To draw closer to the God behind both faiths, I'd converted after he spoke to me through the Book of Mormon. But I saw that as complicating my identity, adding a layer with sometimes awkward overlap. I certainly did not feel I was *more* Jewish.

Messianic Judaism certainly looked a great deal more Jewish than my Latter-day Saint faith. They kept Shabbat at the same times, marked the holidays, ate kosher. Even the soundscape adopted bits of Hebrew: they called Jesus "Yeshua," referred to their pastor as "rabbi." At the same time, however, their theology struck me as mostly in tune with evangelical Protestantism. Their understanding of key concepts like repentance, for example, echoed evangelical interpretations of Paul far more than the notions of repentance I'd learned growing up.

Mormonism doesn't look Jewish. Except for the absence of crosses, a chapel looks typically low-church Protestant. Worship is on Sunday. Though Latter-day Saints take their Sabbath very seriously, they don't keep other Jewish holidays or have much of a religious calendar of their own. And the only dietary restrictions are on things like alcohol, tobacco, and coffee, not pork or shellfish. All the surface culture of Mormonism had

---

1. This is an issue of considerable contention. For further discussion of tensions between mainstream Judaism and the Christian movement known as Messianic Judaism, see the Q&A in the appendix.

been new to me when I converted: I hadn't had the same bridge of comforting familiarity Messianic Jews took such pains to preserve. In Latter-day Saint worship, the most Jewish imagery shows up in the least public, more sacred aspects of the faith—places like the temple and in patriarchal blessings.

That more Christian imagery and language, though, clothed an underlying theology that felt deeply Judaic to me in many ways. The Book of Mormon struck me as so Hebraic in its thought and even language. Mormon understandings of repentance, peoplehood, prophets, and of God's role in history, spoke to my Jewish soul. Mormons believed, unequivocally, in Jesus as Christ. They just didn't feel conventionally *Christian* to me, or carry the same baggage.

And it wasn't just me. Traditional Christian groups didn't warn people against Messianic Jews: from a Christian perspective, their look was different but their theology was familiar. Latter-day Saints, in contrast, existed in dramatic doctrinal tension with other Christian faiths. Other Christians regularly accused Mormons of undervaluing grace, or of being excessively insular and legalistic, or of missing the mark in their faith. Not only did those criticisms suggest a difference in underlying theology—many of them echoed historical Christian criticisms of Jews.

If Messianic Judaism kept the skin of Judaism while offering believers a different heart in the form of conventional Christian theology, Mormonism did the opposite. It seemed to me that the Book of Mormon had given Mormonism a more Judaic heart, wrapped in the skin of the Christian visual culture and soundscape most early Latter-day Saints came from. Many of the Messianic Jews I met were responding to longings like those I had felt, but we'd arrived at quite different places.

Some of them felt I was losing my Jewish identity and encouraged me to embrace more visible Jewish traditions. As it turned out, many were also interested in my experience and what I'd found in the Book of Mormon. When we entered their homes and began teaching them, however, we drew the ire of their congregation's rabbi.

One Friday night, after a Shabbat service, full of Hebrew prayers and synthesizing Judaism and Christianity, he took us into his car to "have a chat with us." I was young and naive enough to believe it would be a friendly conversation.

But, of course, we'd touched a nerve. As missionaries, it seemed generous to us to offer people another way of thinking about God. We knew it took real work for members of our church to create welcoming communities, to pay attention to who was new and to offer their time and emotional support to anyone who passed through. And after all, we would never force anyone to convert. How could it be bad to offer them a choice? Seeing things from that perspective, it was easy to miss how disruptive we could be.

Faith, after all, is not only a matter of personal choice. Faith also offers people belonging—to God, and to a community of people who care about each other's lives. Of course offering a different community, with the potential to divide the community they tended, could easily feel to other religious leaders like a threat.

"Elders, I know all about what you've been doing here. I'm angry with you," the Messianic rabbi said, "for sneaking around in the homes of my congregants and teaching them about your church."

I wanted to show my respect but thought he was out of line for taking the issue into his own hands rather than leaving it to each family. "I'm sorry, sir," I said, "but I thought we were welcome here. We haven't been hiding who we are or what we believe. The members of your congregation are free to learn whatever they want."

He wasn't interested, though, in a discussion about the nature of human choice. "I want you to stop talking to my congregants immediately," he said. His tone was sharp, harsh. "You will regret it if you don't stop."

My blood ran cold. I immediately felt uncomfortable in the car. He wanted the information to go one way: for me to learn about Messianic Judaism. By teaching as well as listening, we'd crossed a line he guarded jealously.

Deep feelings are a valuable part of faith, but if we aren't careful the very depth of our feelings can trap us. I wouldn't have wanted a person of faith to be without passion. But no matter how our beliefs and interests may conflict, we can do better than to threaten each other.

◇ ▢ ◇

Talking with Messianic Jews had seemed like it would be easier, since we had some shared experience. I knew from the beginning that talking with Rockland County's Orthodox Jews would be complicated. Still . . . how could it hurt to start a conversation? My role as a missionary wasn't to push anyone into anything, but to offer. God could decide whether to speak to a person through the Book of Mormon as he had to me, and each person could decide what to do about that if it happened. My role was simply to create opportunities for that process to begin if it was meant to.

I don't think God ever intended to reach every person I spoke with. One day, for example, my companion and I met a haredi Jew taking a jog around a track at a park. Trying to spark curiosity, I said, "Would you be interested in reading the Book of Mormon? It is about ancient Jews who left Jerusalem in the time of the Babylonian exile to come to America."

Well? If God meant for the book to pique this man's interest, I'd given God a moment to work with.

"Give me that book," the man said, taking the copy I offered from my hand. I felt a rush of excitement. Maybe he'd feel what I'd felt, and I'd have the chance to talk through it with someone. Then he addressed me directly. "While your ancestors were worshipping gods of fire; my ancestors were worshipping the living God!" He then proceeded to throw the Book of Mormon into the nearest trash can.

He went back to his jog. I stood there on the track, trying to understand what just happened. What he'd done shocked me, but what he'd said was a different story. As much as I valued the Book of Mormon, I couldn't fault the man for his show of pride in the truths he knew. Even though my ancestors were also Jews, I was not offended by what he said about mine. I respected his passionate conviction. For him, if it wasn't Judaism, it was paganism. He was sincerely trying to worship God as revealed to Moses.

When you're a missionary, you'll miss a lot if you spend all your time wanting people to see things just like you do. The fire of divine presence is there in so many eyes: even those with nothing but disdain for what you might have to say!

Not all of the haredim wrote me off so quickly. One day, we were contacting people in a park in Monsey, New York, when we met a man named Yaakov.

As I recall, I asked him the very same question: "Would you be interested in reading the Book of Mormon, about ancient Israelites who came to America during the time of the Babylonian exile?"

"No, thanks," Yaakov said, " I am committed to Judaism."

My companion interjected. "Well, Elder Olson here is a Jew!" he said.

As it happened, this was during Passover. Yaakov was carrying a huge piece of matzah, the unleavened bread Jews eat by commandment during Passover to remind us of the exodus from Egypt. It was different than the crisp, factory-made squares I had grown up with, though: he clearly made his own matzah at home. He immediately stopped what he was doing and offered some to me.

I took a bite of the matzah. There is something sacred about breaking bread with another person. "Thank you," I told him.

Then Yaakov said, "Elder Olson, would you like to learn more about your own religion?"

I said, "Absolutely."

We began a friendship that lasted for years. We compared family trees: Grandma Gilda was a Rosenberg and Yaakov had Rosenbergs in his family tree, too. So many records in Europe were lost in the Holocaust that it's hard to trace our families back, but we liked at least wondering if we were related. I kept in touch with him even after my mission, tried to visit whenever I was in New York. Yaakov was the one who would later recommend a friend of mine to study at Ohr Somayach Yeshiva in Jerusalem. He had the sincerest love for every Jew. He was not offended in the least that I had converted to the restored gospel. From my perspective, I had gone through a complex religious transition. From his haredi perspective, the Reform Judaism of my early life and my Mormonism were not so different. A Torah-observant lifestyle was more important than beliefs, and in either case, I was a Jew who was not keeping the Torah as he understood it. If I was ready, he was simply and patiently willing to help me return to observant Judaism.

The fire of divine presence is in so many people's eyes. In Yaakov's, I could see God's love shining.

◇ ▢ ◇

Many of the Jews I spoke with in Rockland County were people I met in passing, at parks, on streets, in neighborhoods. Avinoam was different. He was an Israeli Jew who'd been raised Orthodox but belonged to a Reform congregation when I met him. His wife, Lena, was a Latter-day Saint from Trinidad.

Together, they were making things work in their mixed-faith family. Lena occasionally attended Sunday services and cherished her Latter-day Saint beliefs but also shared in Jewish observances and traditions. Avinoam, for his part, was not trying to create the kind of Orthodox household he'd grown up in. He had left much of his Torah observance and ate bacon, milk with meat, and so on. He honored the Sabbath but did not keep it in the Orthodox way.

After hearing about each other, both Avinoam and I were eager to meet. He had my companion and me over for a Friday night Shabbat meal with his family. I loved hearing the Hebrew again, soaking in the sound of the prayers, and savoring the chance to welcome in the Sabbath I'd grown up with. I missed my people. I missed my language. I missed my Torah. Each time we sang the Havdalah Shabbat prayer, it all came rushing back.

I loved Avi's Israeli accent. He still read his Bible; it was entirely in Hebrew. I loved hearing his stories of being raised on a religious kibbutz, a communal settlement. Avi was a gracious host, and willing to have me share my thoughts about the Book of Mormon with him. Having married Lena, the basics of the faith weren't new to him. Still, he expressed appreciation for having a fellow Jew who had "insight" into the world of the Latter-day Saints.

Avi and Lena were raising their two children in Judaism, even though having Jewish ancestry on the father's rather than the mother's side meant they were not considered as born Jewish under many understandings of Jewish law. The Conservative Rabbi they had initially worshipped with wanted the children to formally convert to Judaism in order to have bar and bat mitzvahs. This offended Avi, so they started to attend a Reform synagogue. Since 1983, the Reform movement accepted patrilineal descent, so the new congregation treated the children as Jews without having to go through a formal conversion process.

Lena was supportive. Avi was a child of Holocaust survivors, so it was very important for him to pass on his faith to the next generation. But he wasn't threatened by our presence as missionaries. While he didn't want his children to attend church with us, he allowed us to develop friendly relationships with them.

One famous missionary story in the Book of Mormon features a man named Ammon who visits his people's traditional enemies. Rather than starting his work by preaching to them, he offers to become a servant. For Lena and Avi's family, it seemed like the best approach was not to focus on teaching, as we usually did, but simply to serve Avi and his family. At the time, he was working to transform his front and back yards into beautiful gardens. I promised my companion and I would help. He took us up on the offer.

The hours we spent working with Avi meant a lot to me. Missionaries are expected to devote a certain number of hours each week to some local service opportunity, and getting to spend them in support of a family like Lena and Avi's felt to me like a good choice. My companion, who was a brand-new missionary, was less convinced. He wanted to find new people to teach, and was eager to focus all his efforts on religious conversion. "Why are we doing so much service for Avi's family?" he asked me. "It's a waste of time. He's not even interested in learning the Gospel. You just like to help him because he's a Jew and you're a Jew."

He wasn't wrong about my sense of connection to Avi as a Jew and to a mixed-religion family, but that didn't mean we were wasting time. "Whether Avi joins the Church or not is not the point," I told him. "Service is not an opportunity to teach. It's an opportunity to love."

We spent countless hours moving rocks and plants around Avi's large yard to accomplish his vision. It looked like a Japanese garden. So organized, so ornate. Working alongside each other, sharing stories and ideas and memories along the way, we'd built something beautiful and balanced. I knew conversion could change lives. But relationships between people of different faiths also contribute to the great whole of humanity. Avi knew I loved him, whether he joined the Church or not. And I felt the love and respect he had for us.

Like my companion, I'd started my mission eager to find

people who were open to experiences with the Book of Mormon and Latter-day Saints beliefs like I'd had. In particular, I'd hoped to reach the Jewish communities of New York and New Jersey. After building a garden with Avi, though, it felt less and less like that's what God wanted me to do. I was at peace to simply serve my fellow Jews.

CHAPTER TEN

GOD'S MYSTERIOUS WAYS

◇

Why was I on a mission? That was something I asked myself more and more as the months passed. Not as a complaint, but as a spiritual inquiry. It seemed clear that God wasn't in a hurry for every person I met to embrace the restored gospel. I knew God could speak through the Book of Mormon, but it seemed so rare for him to tell people it was his book as directly and dramatically as he had told me. Maybe he would have for some, if they'd been more prepared to stop and listen. Or maybe not: maybe God wanted some people to live as Latter-day Saints and others to live as Jews or Catholics or Buddhists. God is certainly big enough to work within the pieces of truth in all kinds of traditions. He has his own plans for everybody.

Maybe God wanted me on a mission for the sake of the people who were looking for something and found a new faith through us: maybe I was there for Maya and Shiva, for Jeff and Sharon. And maybe God also wanted me on a mission to bless other lives: for families like the Nolans, or for Lena and Avi. And finally, maybe God wanted me on a mission for the way it would change me. Maybe he'd sent me from Arizona out to New Jersey and New York to grow in confidence and to be blessed by the paths I would cross.

Many meetings on my mission certainly didn't seem like coincidences. They felt designed to offer me or someone else an opportunity for growth or change.

Why, for example, had I been called to start my mission in Jersey City? Neither the apostle who matched my application with a mission, nor the mission president who prayed over where to assign me knew that my most powerful association with Jersey City was that it was where Rick Ross, who had put me through his hazing-like "deprogramming" process, had his office.

Was it coincidence? Or were our paths meant to cross a second time?

I decided to look him up. Sure enough, I found his name in the Yellow Pages. My mission companions had heard this part of my story before and were a little taken aback. Was it really a good idea to willingly go meet with someone who'd gotten paid to attack their religion? For me, though, going willingly was part of the point. We'd met before on Rick's terms. I wanted to see him again when it was my choice.

When my companions asked if he was going to shake our testimonies, I found myself replying with a peaceful confidence. "No," I said. " The Book of Mormon is true." What else mattered?

So, I called him and introduced myself. "Hi, this is Elder Jason Olson, of The Church of Jesus Christ of Latter-day Saints. You came to my home in Scottsdale, Arizona last year and now I'm a full-time missionary. I'd like to know if my companions and I can visit you."

Rick hesitated for just a moment. Then he said, "Sure. Please stop by."

By the time we sat down with Rick in his office in downtown Jersey City, my companions were feeling pretty anxious. They probably thought I was crazy—which gave them one thing, at least, in common with Rick. He remembered me. He was surprised that I was already a missionary, not to mention that I was assigned to the area he worked in.

After quick greetings, I got to the point. "We decided to come here to simply leave our testimonies of the Gospel of Jesus Christ so you can know that God sent us to you."

"I think your religion is a fraud," Rick said.

But I bore him my testimony anyway. I had told him about my beliefs before, but before it had been to defend myself. Now I was offering him my testimony as a gift. No one was paying me to do so, and I wasn't going to press the issue. I just believed that everyone, even a guy who had been so hard on me, deserved whatever chance I could offer for an encounter with God.

I don't know if my visit made any difference for Rick. But I'm glad God sent me to Rick's city. It meant closure, at least, for me.

In Rockland County, I got a different chance to meet with a figure from my past once again. Tovia Singer of Outreach Judaism, the man who had unknowingly launched my whole experience, was based in Monsey, New York. I found him in the Yellow Pages.

Was it coincidence? Or were our paths meant to cross a second time?

I was so struck by finding him there, I immediately told my companion the whole story. We agreed that I would call him to set an appointment. This time, I was the one who was nervous. Rick Ross hadn't felt like a serious threat to me because there was so little power in his methods. Rabbi Singer was different. I remembered the spiritual weight in his words. His commitment to Judaism was compelling. Still, if the coincidence was actually providence, I should go. Maybe for him. Maybe for me.

When we arrived at Rabbi Singer's office, he was gracious. It was evident that he had met with Christian missionaries many times. He didn't act offended or threatened by our presence. There was no anxiety there. So I just told him my story: how his words, in a way, had brought me here.

He wasn't upset, but something in the story moved him. "Jason," he said. "Hashem has brought you back to me." There were tears in his eyes.

Hashem. Hebrew for "the name." It's the way many Jews, especially Orthodx Jews, refer to God, not wanting to take his name in vain. A word I'd heard from Rabbi Raphael's lips countless times.

From Rabbi Singer's perspective, as from Yaakov's, I had gone astray. I was, perhaps, in a state of rebellion. Well? So were the children of Israel more than once in the Torah.

He asked about my scripture study. Wanted to know if I was still studying the books of the Hebrew Bible. I was still reading passages, of course, though the truth was that having four volumes of scripture made it harder to focus on any single one.

"Which version of the Hebrew Bible are you reading?" he asked me.

"King James," I told him.

"Well, why don't you read your own Bible in Hebrew?" he said. "Since you don't even know your own Bible and your own language, how can you give your life to the Mormons? At least give Judaism a chance."

That didn't feel fair to me. I might not have trained as a rabbi, but my conversion had hardly been casual. "Rabbi," I explained, "I did give Judaism a chance. I studied with an Orthodox rabbi for three years in high school. Still, I couldn't shake my testimony of Jesus being the Messiah. I know Jesus Christ is the God of Israel, the God of Abraham, Isaac, and Jacob."

I knew this might shock him and would sound blasphemous. But as a missionary, I was used to testifying. I didn't have the language yet for a sophisticated dialogue: I just knew how to share.

Rabbi Singer was gracious about it. "I appreciate your sharing that with me," he said. "But I want you to really study

Judaism. You need to attend a Yeshiva and give yourself to full-time study of the Torah. After you do this, you'll be able to make up your mind."

I don't know what about full-time missionary service made it look like I hadn't made up my mind, but I was happy to show respect for Jewish learning, which I still valued. "It would be great to study in a Yeshiva and learn more about Judaism," I said.

"Well, just take off your name tag," he said. "Stop your mission right now and study in the Yeshiva here in Monsey!"

I told him, of course, that I couldn't. That I had made a commitment.

He understood. He still insisted on giving me a Chumash, a printed version of the five books of Moses. A gift and a reminder.

After that visit, I found myself turning more frequently to the Hebrew prophets and reading their words more intensely. As I poured through the writings of Moses, Isaiah, Jeremiah, Ezekiel, Zechariah, Amos, and others, one theme in particular stood out to me. It was the call to return: to God, to the Torah. To the land of Israel. *Had Hashem returned me to Rabbi Singer after all?*

When I was called to New Jersey and New York, I had thought I would get to help some of my fellow Jews convert as I had. Over the course of my mission, though, I had felt again and again that wasn't God's primary intention for me. Or for them.

After meeting with Rabbi Singer, my thoughts began to turn more and more toward Israel. I began to feel that maybe one reason God wanted to preserve Jews as Jews was in order to gather them to their promised land. Growing up with Israelis in our congregation, and flying an Israeli flag, I'd felt a certain connection to the Jewish state. But it was as a Mormon missionary that I really started to feel the pull of Zionism.

CHAPTER ELEVEN

LONGING FOR ZION

◇

Once again Rabbi Singer had sparked something in me. Through my renewed study of the Hebrew prophets, I had grown more and more interested in the themes of exile and return: what the rabbis called *kibbutz galuyyot*. I began to embrace a strong Zionist view of Jewish history, the Jewish present, and the Jewish future. I just didn't have a clear idea of where I might fit into it as a Mormon and a Jew.

For Latter-day Saints, the term *Zion* is not typically associated with the state of Israel. Early Mormons were deeply interested in the Biblical concept of the literal gathering of Israel. Missionaries in the nineteenth century didn't just share a new set of doctrinal beliefs: they encouraged converts to migrate to Latter-day Saint population centers to help build up an American Zion. Over time, the aspiration to build Zion came to refer to a holy way of living, with unity and care for the poor, wherever on earth the Saints gathered.

I had some opportunities to study Latter-day Saint history on my mission, though, and there are intriguing connections between the early history of the Church and the idea of a Jewish Zion. Ideas of gathering a spiritual Israel existed alongside rather than replacing ideas about specifically Jewish exile. As the early Latter-day Saints worked to build their first temple, they also hired a Hebrew teacher to come and introduce them to Biblical Hebrew. Like Rabbi Singer, they had felt there were insights to be gained from reading scripture in its original language.

When Joseph Smith gave the dedicatory prayer for the Kirtland temple in 1836, he prayed specifically for the Jews and for Jerusalem. "We therefore ask thee to have mercy upon the children of Jacob," he asked God, "that Jerusalem, from this hour, may begin to be redeemed; and the yoke of bondage may begin to be broken off from the house of David; and the children of Judah may begin to return to the lands which thou didst give to Abraham, their father" (Doctrine & Covenants 109:62–64).

In 1840, a Latter-day Saint apostle named Orson Hyde was sent on an unusual mission: one to visit Jewish communities in Europe en route to Jerusalem, where he offered a prayer dedicating the land for the return of the Jews. Along the way, Hyde stopped in New Jersey. Yet another crossing of paths: I was in the same place as the Jerusalem-bound apostle.

While he was in New Jersey, Hyde wrote asking Joseph Smith a question: should any Jews who converted go to Jerusalem or gather to the American Zion the Saints were helping to build? The question felt particularly relevant to me. Joseph said converted Jews should come and join with the rest of the Saints.[1] Part of that may have been practical: whatever their beliefs about a coming gathering to Jerusalem, Latter-day Saint settlements had an immediate need for the talents and contributions of any converts. At the same time, it revealed something deeper: while Jewish tradition emphasizes a single promised land, Joseph Smith believed in at least two.

I didn't really grasp it at the time, but the Book of Mormon's

---

1. The Joseph Smith Papers, "Letter to Quorum of the Twelve, 15 December 1840," 7, josephsmithpapers.org

depiction of the Americas as another promised land overtly applied to the Jews it warned people against persecuting. Orson Hyde and Joseph Smith prayed for the day when Jews would be able to make homes in Israel, but without viewing Israel as the only promised land. Certainly, from the Book of Mormon's perspective, America should be a place of peace for Jacob's scattered descendants, *another* "Jewish homeland."

As a missionary, my focus was supposed to be firmly on a more abstract Zion. My job was to gather people from a personal exile into the warmth and connection of the Church. Within my new faith's teachings, though, the more literal possibilities hadn't disappeared: Latter-day Saints still imagine the day might come when we migrate together to build holy cities again. Those dreams are just dormant, waiting for their time.

After my meeting with Rabbi Singer, a more Zionist dream of a promised land was also waking within me. My friendship with Avi was definitely an influence, reminding me how it might feel to share the rhythms of Jewish life in a Jewish land. The words of ancient prophets seemed likewise to be calling me toward Israel. Whatever the causes, I became hungry, thirsty, desperate to experience the land of my forefathers and foremothers, the Holy Land.

My mission came to an end with that hunger. During the two years I served, I'd gotten to know people from many backgrounds and cultures. I'd had a few amazing experiences bringing others into the Church of Jesus Christ. I'd had other wonderful experiences of service and personal connection.

I also had encounters with many different kinds of Jews who broadened my understanding of Jewish identity.

I was changed as a person. I was changed as a Latter-day Saint. I was changed as a Jew.

◇ ▢ ◇

In July 2006, I was released from my mission. Rather than

going straight back home to Scottsdale, I went first to Chicago to visit my maternal grandparents. It was the last time I would see my grandmother: she died later that year.

Grandma Gilda still hoped with all her heart I would marry a nice Jewish girl. It was important to her that Jewish identity be passed on down the generations. I don't think she regretted my mother's marriage outside the faith, but she had witnessed and worried over the prospect of assimilation into the wider Christian culture and the loss of Jewish memory that might lead to. Grandma Gilda was trying to keep the Jewish people, her people, going. She had clothed me in the tallit, had handed down the Torah scroll to me as symbols of that hope. For her, Torah observance was not at the heart of what it meant to be Jewish. Instead, Judaism was about group identification, an identity and a set of loyalties not to be given up.

"I'm so relieved you're done with your mission," she told me. "Are you going to be Jewish now?"

"I'll always be Jewish," I said. "But I don't know what you want me to do. I still believe in Jesus. I can't shake that faith. I'll never be fully accepted in the Jewish community with that belief."

My great-uncle tried to lighten the mood. "So you're a Mormon now, eh?" he said.

"Yep," I said. "I just finished my mission."

"How many wives are ya gonna have now?" he asked with a smirk.

The answer was one (assuming I found somebody). But he knew that. Latter-day Saints had performed plural marriages for about sixty years. Jokes and barbs about polygamy had lasted twice that long since the Church gave up the practice and were still going strong.

For some Latter-day Saints, polygamy was a sore point. A lot were just tired of getting teased or harassed about it. Others couldn't make sense of why something so foreign to Western tradition had happened in the Church. For me, though, the polygamy in Mormon history was oddly reassuring. Where other Christians had treated Jews as backward, early Mormons had revived an ancient Semitic practice. Even though polygamy among Ashkenazi Jews was banned by Rabbenu Gershom, known as the "Light of the Exile," in the 11th century, the early Latter-day Saint acceptance of a marriage system Europeans had stigmatized was not a scandal. If anything, for me, it was one more sign that they cared about the roots of Abrahamic religion. That Mormons could have a unique affinity for Jews and Muslims.

So I answered my great-uncle's question with another one. "Well, how many wives did Jacob have?" I asked. "A long time ago, Jews were polygamists too!"

He laughed. "You've got a point. You have got a point! Welcome back home, Jason. We've missed you."

Our family's patriarch, Papa Al, worked as before to extend an olive branch. He asked me for a copy of the Book of Mormon. He told me he supported me in whatever decisions I made going forward.

In my generation of Americans, we really value affirmation. I can see why: it feels good to know someone you care about is willing to acknowledge you thought hard about a decision and respects you enough to support it. At the same time, though, I think there's a lot of love in a person's willingness to bring up difficult subjects and share their own perspective. My grandpa's support meant everything to me—but grandma's insistence that I should keep the Jewish people going meant everything, too.

I didn't exactly look like I was still doing anything to contribute to the Jewish community. But I confided in her about how I was thinking about Israel. She lit up at that: she made me promise I would at least try to go. It was one of the last things we talked about. Something I would remember, a few months later at her burial, as my family members and I threw dirt from the land of Israel onto her casket and I wished my grandmother goodbye.

I had a lot to figure out in my own life. When I went on a mission, my parents had worried it would lead me away from college and throw my whole professional life off track, but that's not what typically happens. Missionary service teaches discipline, tenacity, and a sense of purpose. As soon as possible, I was off to BYU and throwing myself into my studies. I took Rabbi Singer's invitation seriously: I signed up for four Hebrew classes my first year at BYU, eager to build skills in both Biblical and modern Hebrew. Wondering how I could do what Grandma Gilda had asked me to do.

◇ ◻ ◇

I liked BYU. It was good to be back on campus with friends like Shea and Matt after all our missions (Dave wasn't back from his yet). It was good to be around people who shared the same religion, who I could talk to about my spiritual experiences. Like Judaism, though, Mormonism was more than just a religion. There were cultures that had grown up around the religion. New Jersey's Latter-day Saint congregations had a more multicultural feel. BYU's culture was more strongly shaped by the early Mormon pioneers who'd come to Utah. There was a lot to like in the culture. There was a lot I admired. But it didn't feel like it was mine.

Maybe that's why I felt drawn to people who weren't from that Utah pioneer culture either. In my modern Hebrew class, I made friends with an Israeli classmate. Lama was from a Palestinian Christian family, and unlike the vast majority of BYU students, she was not a Latter-day Saint. Despite being in an unfamiliar culture, however, she was confident and direct, unafraid to tell you when she disagreed. That openness, even bluntness, appealed to me: Ashkenazi Jews run blunt ourselves! I remembered Farooq telling me that Jews and Arabs are cousins, and talking with Lama, that felt so true. I felt comfortable with the shared approaches of our respective cultures, and was interested in learning more about of her perspective as an Israeli and a Palestinian.

It was clear from the beginning that our perspectives on Israel were very different. For me, it was important to know that there was a place in the world where the Jewish people had some control over its own fate. I have never supported every action Israeli governments take, but I support the state of Israel. Like most Palestinians, Lama was more focused on the struggles of Palestinians both in Israel and the occupied territories of Gaza and the West bank. She had a much more negative view of Zionism.

I still loved talking with her. She was smart. She was funny. I valued her perspective, even though I came from a different position. I also felt like I could relate to her in a different way than I related to many of my other BYU peers. That was important to me.

In my Biblical Hebrew class, I met another unexpected friend when one of the students walked in wearing a tallit and a kippah. I was surprised: there was a Jewish community in Salt Lake, but not really in Provo. I didn't know any Orthodox Jews lived there.

It turned out David Luna wasn't Orthodox. His Jewish parents had converted to Mormonism before he was born. Though he was raised in the restored gospel, he'd remained connected to his family's roots and was trying to find his own way of holding on to Jewish identity within his faith. I really admired David. He was a dynamic, engaging, insatiably curious person. Like my grandfather, he'd served in the United States military. In my eyes, his two combat tours to Iraq with the Marines made him an American hero.

While I didn't wear a tallit or anything of the kind, I was glad David Luna had. His choice to wear outer symbols of Judaism had helped me recognize something inside of him. A kindred spirit. We both felt the pull of Judaism like a gravitational force. And, however frustrating it may have been to Lama, that pull manifested itself at least in part in a thirst for Israel. We both felt yearning to return to the land of Israel. We wanted to experience it for ourselves and contribute to Jewish life there.

I wonder how many people like us have passed through Brigham Young University. In my time there I met more: people with Jewish ancestry, practicing Mormonism while working to carry on Jewish memory in their own ways. At one stake conference, I saw someone else carrying a tallit bag with an image of the Holy City of Jerusalem. Of course I had to talk with him. His name was Aaron. Like David Luna, his Jewish parents had converted to Mormonism. Like David, he felt the pull of his Jewish roots. Aaron, David, and I started getting together every Saturday evening at Aaron's sister's house. Three Jewish-Mormon musketeers, gathering almost like on Shabbat.

People may have seen David and Aaron as a little eccentric, but on BYU campus, they didn't seem to mind. For the most part, Latter-day Saints don't have a problem with Jewish Mormons still being a little Jewish. They tend to recognize the affinity between the traditions: there are enough depictions of Judaism in American culture that they can see things they recognize. At BYU, Latter-day Saints with intellectual ties to Judaism worked to show students the beauty in the faith and its tradition. I remember going to a Passover seder held by a religion professor named Victor Ludlow, and Rosh Hashanah and Sukkot celebrations led by Hebrew instructor Monica Richards and the university's Hebrew club. Ancient Judaism, of course, is at the root of all Christian scripture—but historically, Christians hadn't always looked for insights through present Judaism in the ways I saw in Latter-day Saints at BYU. What was different?

For most of history, Christians have found ways to make a distinction between the children of Israel in scripture and the Jewish community that remained after Jesus' death. It was entirely possible for them to honor the former and hate the latter, because they believed in an idea called supersessionism: that the Christian covenant replaced the covenants God made through Abraham and Moses. In historical Christianity, then, Christians became the new chosen people with little need for the old things, which had passed away.

Because of the way the story of the Crucifixion was told, in particular, it was easy to cast Jews not only as backward for rejecting the new light of Christianity, but as fundamentally traitorous. Judas had betrayed Christ. By extension, Jews were seen as betraying the Christian world. And Christians were trying to build a new and better world: one with better care for the sick, with food for the hungry, where love and righteousness displaced sin. Medieval monks and nuns accomplished some wonderful things in promoting public service and learning.

But any social or political system with dreams of a better world ends up needing an explanation for why the world isn't as perfect yet as ideology promised it would be. Communist countries, for example, regularly tore themselves apart in paranoid searches for hidden counter-revolutionaries: people still clinging to the old ways after the new order was beginning.

Over the centuries, Christendom had struggled to understand its own failures and placed the blame on Jews, who were seen as rejecting the new order by failing to accept Jesus as the Messiah and continuing to witness that the world is unredeemed. Operating from a frame of resentment, it wasn't much of a stretch for centuries of Christians to imagine Jews in one conspiracy or another to plot their world's destruction.

The foundational Latter-day Saint view of Judaism was different, I suspect, because the religion's fundamental vision of time is different. Most Christians had seen time as a forward progression with Christianity replacing Judaism, the present eclipsing an vestigial past. Latter-day Saints' founding belief that Christianity had lost something essential challenged that view. Latter-day Saints were convinced instead that a restoration of ancient truths was needed. That the past held real power.

The obligation to remember, which is so important in Judaism, is also a major theme in the Book of Mormon. Book of Mormon peoples hold on to their sense of belonging within God's covenant with the House of Israel long after they leave the promised land. In their new home, they immediately go to work building a temple. They maintain a priesthood. They talk about remembering the captivity of their fathers in ways that sound like the Passover haggadah.

Though keeping Passover and other Jewish holidays mentioned in the Bible isn't a Latter-day Saint practice, the themes of the Jewish calendar resonated so easily with Latter-day Saints. Certainly, there were people at BYU who valued my conversion primarily as a sign of the truth and value of their faith—but I also met plenty who felt like I'd brought something valuable with me, something they could learn from. Latter-day Saints who believed that God's ongoing relationship with Jews could still bless the earth, as God had promised Abraham.

Latter-day Saint theology, and a Latter-day Saint view of time, left room for Jewish covenant. And so people like Aaron, David, and me, who embraced Latter-day Saint theology, still tried to make sense of what that covenant might mean. As we talked and dreamed together, our motivation fed off each other and our resolve grew: we made plans to go to Israel, someday soon, together.

◇ ◻ ◇

At the same time, I was getting to know Lama better and we were talking more about Israel. For her, my fascination with the land was deeply suspect. Like many Arab Israelis, Lama had a strong distaste for Zionism. She felt it viscerally, to the point that she'd been unable to bring herself to come back to Latter-day Saint meetings after her first visit with friends because everyone had sung a hymn that used the word Zion, again and again. Even knowing Latter-day Saints use the word in a different way, the experience left a bad taste in her mouth. She was happy to talk with me about Israel, but thought I was naive in my perspective.

Her reactions made me a little defensive: why should she be so opposed to the connection I felt? Growing up, we'd always displayed the Israeli flag alongside the American flag in our synagogue. There were Israelis in our congregation. For me, Israel was a bright hope shining out of a dark history.

Take just my ancestors' village of Bogopol. The Jewish community there was targeted in pogroms in 1881 and 1905 (the year Papa Al's parents left). During the Russian Revolution, the White Army spread anti-Semitic propoganda and still more Jews were beaten, robbed, murdered. By the time the Nazis came, the Jewish population in Bogopol and the neighboring towns had already dropped from around 40% in 1900 to less than 20%. In just four years under the Nazis, about 90% of the remaining Jews were murdered. And not only in concentration camps. Thousands were gathered onto a farm and massacred. Others were crowded into a clubhouse and burned alive.[2]

The foundation of a Jewish state in Israel, building out from the handful of Jewish settlements that had always remained, had restored a sense of collective dignity for Jews around the world who had felt powerless to prevent tragedy after tragedy. Decades after the Holocaust, Jews from many countries continued to look to Israel for hope as they faced discrimination in the workplace, as their places of worship remained targets for vandalism and violence. Distant relatives of mine in Argentina had finally decided to gather to Israel after a bombing there. As an American coming of age in the 1990s and early 2000s, I felt relatively safe—but never indifferent to

2. "Pervomaisk," jewishvirtuallibrary.org

the ongoing plight of the world's Jews.

That story, though, isn't the only story. I understood that Lama had a different kind of connection to the land as both her home and her ancestors' home. I appreciated her willingness to share her thoughts with me, even across our differences. Of course, hearing her thoughts didn't give me access to all the feelings and associations behind them. It's so hard to really understand what another person is talking about when your sympathies stand right in the way of their point of view. We'd go back and forth. Trying to sort out differences of opinion wrapped up in totally different histories and perspectives. Many of the stories about Jewish Israelis that she grew up with involved disruption instead of refuge. Of course we saw things differently.

It was easier to grow in understanding for David and Aaron, even as I began to recognize important differences between their perspectives and mine. I was a convert to the Church of Jesus Christ of Latter-day Saints, so I had all the positive associations of finding a community that embraced me when I was a stranger. What's more, my mission assignment in New Jersey and New York had put me in a place where people lived side by side with plenty of Jews. Anti-Semitism has deep roots, and no nation has entirely eliminated it as a threat, but in New Jersey in the early 2000s, prejudice against Jews was the exception rather than the rule. I hadn't really known it among Latter-day Saints.

Aaron's experience as a missionary in Spain was totally different. Spain had a fascist government for decades after World War II and conspiracy theories about Jews had been a regular part of public discussion during the same postwar period when many countries had worked to do away with antisemitism in their cultures. Because of that history, Aaron regularly met people who were openly hostile to Jews. Some of them were members of the Church. During one of the hardest periods of his mission, Aaron had spent all day every day assigned to serve alongside an anti-Semitic companion. One day, Aaron found a swastika drawn on his scriptures. I could hardly imagine how that would have felt. His mission companion, who he was supposed to be able to trust and rely on as they worked together, had drawn it, desecrating God's word with a symbol of white supremacy and mass murder.

That had a huge impact on Aaron. If I longed to maintain my connection to Judaism, Aaron felt driven to reclaim his. On my mission, I'd deepened my connection to the Hebrew prophets; Aaron had dived into the books of the Torah, aiming to rebuild his Jewish identity from the roots. He, too, was drawn to the state of Israel. He had a worn copy of Theodore Herzl's utopian novel *Old Land, New Land* on his shelf. One Saturday night, he insisted on having us watch the film *Munich* together, considering the tensions and violence that still accompanied a Jewish state. Aaron wanted to fight the anti-Semitism he'd experienced by holding onto Jewish identity with immovable resolve.

David had his own reasons for turning to Judaism, his own things to look for in Israel. When I first heard about his United States military service, I could only see it in heroic tones. But that's not the only way David saw himself. In Iraq, David's ideals had been stripped down at times to loyalty to the Marines serving with him. Not all of them had survived.

David opened up to me more and more during our Saturday evenings together. One night, as we talked, feeling the closeness that comes with shared dreams, David had also told me about the wartime memory that haunted him most.

He and his Marines had been on patrol in a Humvee, bouncing down a desert road in such bad shape that some of the bumps almost rattled them out of their seats. In the distance, they saw an Iraqi man walking out into the road. The man was dressed in long robes, and struck David as looking very religious. He waved them over, wanting to talk. As the group's leader, David felt like it was his job to approach him. The man reached toward David, his robe fell open, and for a moment David swore the man was wearing explosives. David had reacted with swift, lethal force, drawing his knife and stabbing the man—only to find he hadn't been a threat after all. There were no explosives. David had killed an innocent man, whose only mistake had been reaching out to embrace him.

He had only been trying to protect his Marines. But shedding innocent blood, even through a mistake in judgment, left him with lingering moral scars. After that day, David was searching for something. A spiritual power to hold onto. Some kind of healing for the tumult within him. Some salve for the unseen wounds of war.

We ate together. We talked together. We dreamed of Zion. What were we looking for?

PART THREE

TWO ZIONS

CHAPTER TWELVE

ALIYAH

◇

As it happened, Israel's national cantorial choir visited Salt Lake City that year. This group, consisting of some of Israel's top religious singers, had been invited to perform at the Church's Conference Center in Salt Lake City, where the Tabernacle Choir at Temple Square regularly performed. Of course I attended.

They performed traditional Jewish songs and psalms, as well as modern Israeli pieces. Listening to them reminded me of the time I spent preparing for my bar mitzvah, learning the trope and chanting from the Torah. Their voices were beautiful; their Hebrew gorgeous. The climax was their rendition of "Hatikvah," Israel's national anthem:

> As long as in the heart, within,
> A Jewish soul still yearns,
> And onward, towards the ends of the east,
> an eye still gazes toward Zion;
>
> Our hope is not yet lost,
> The hope of two thousand years,
> To be a free nation in our land,
> The land of Zion and Jerusalem.

When I heard their clear, powerful voices extending those words of hope, I could feel my desire to see Israel rising within. I felt compelled to return to the land.

After the performance in the Conference Center, I introduced myself to the cantors, letting them know that I, too, am Jewish. They greeted me warmly and even invited me to come to their hotel to recite the Shacharit prayers with them the next morning.

"I would love to," I said. "Thank you for the invitation."

When I met them at the hotel conference room, the dozen of them were assembled, like angels, in their prayer shawls and tefillin. Together, we faced east toward Jerusalem, and they prayed in the most beautiful Israeli Hebrew I had ever heard. I really thought I was hearing voices from heaven.

I felt the Spirit like a wind, rushing through the room, transporting me to the holy city, the heartbeat of my faith as a Jew and as a Latter-day Saint. I thought of how our ancestors worshipped in temple days. I didn't think the songs of Levite choirs would have felt very different, no matter how they sounded.

Sometimes people use the word *transported* to talk about the way music moves them. That word exactly captured my experience. I can believe in a spiritual transportation to Jerusalem because of how I felt in that moment. I have no problem believing some of the Jewish mystics went there in spirit, or accepting some deep kind of truth in the story of Muhammed's night ride.[1] The cantors' prayers resonated in me, and in that moment, I made up my mind. "I'm going to make aliyah," I told them. I wanted to do more than see Israel: I wanted to settle down there.

Wonderful, they told me. They invited me to visit when I came. There was no doubt in my mind at that moment that

---

1. Known as the *mir'aj*, this was one of the most important mystical experiences of the prophet Muhammad. He claims he was transported to Jerusalem by his night steed, where he ascended to heaven to meet with prophets, angels, and God.

these were my brothers. I didn't know if Israel would offer me a home, but I knew I had to try.

◇ □ ◇

The BYU Jerusalem Center had been closed for several years at the time due to a period of unrest called the Second Intifada. I was thrilled to hear, around the time of the cantors' visit, that it would reopen at the beginning of 2007. I immediately applied to attend. So did many other BYU students: study in Jerusalem had always been popular with students interested in Hebrew, Arabic, international relations, history, or art. Far from discouraging applicants, the Jerusalem Center's extended closing seemed to have created a pent-up demand. Since demand was greater than availability, they selected students through a lottery. Hopes and prayers notwithstanding, I didn't make it into that year's class.

That was understandable, of course. It was a matter of random chance. But I was still crushed. I felt so strongly that I needed to get to Israel, but I hadn't made the cut through the traditional Jewish route or this new Mormon one.

I decided to reach out to Rabbi Raphael and see if there was anything he could do. He didn't ask me whether I still believed in Jesus. That wasn't important to him. He believed that my soul was Jewish. Even though I had embraced The Church of Jesus Christ of Latter-day Saints, even though I had served as a missionary, he felt I needed to go home. He believed there was something in the land of Israel that went deeper than human categorizations of faith or nation. My rabbi believed in scattered sparks of light in the descendants of Abraham, Isaac, and Jacob. He believed in a spiritual power in the land of Israel that could repair those sparks. My sparks.

Whatever he wrote on my behalf, it worked! I got a seat on the next ten-day Birthright trip that summer. I was going to Israel.

◇ ◻ ◇

Ever since I'd promised Grandma Gilda, three months before her death, that I would go to Israel, my mom had been looking forward to it. Working through the Jewish Community Center (JCC) in Scottsdale, my mom helped me get in contact with the Jewish Agency for Israel and their *shaliach*, or emissary. Before I had ever set foot in Israel, we made arrangements for me to get housing at one of the country's many immigrant absorption centers, in a town called Ra'anana. I also got set up with an internship at The Center for Jewish-Arab Economic Development. It would only last a few months, but I figured that would give me some time to get oriented to the new country and find a school to enroll in. I was confident I would find my place.

Back at BYU, a lot of my friends were less excited about what I was planning. Shea and Matt (and Dave Thaxton, who was out on his mission) had always been good to me. They'd talked through my questions when we were teenagers, they'd given me the Book of Mormon, they'd comforted me through tough times and offered their homes and friendship as places of refuge when life got hard.

They couldn't understand why I wanted to live in Israel. For them, life had a simple enough script: you chose the right and said no to temptations through high school, you found a nice Latter-day Saint girl in college and got married, then you supported a family, passed on faith to the next generation, and used your talents to serve the community. It was a good, simple life. From their perspective, God had put me on the path to that nice, steady life . . . and moving to Israel wasn't part of the picture. At best, it was an eccentric distraction. At worst, I was risking leaving the Latter-day Saint path altogether by investing so much in my identity as a Jew. They couldn't understand what I was feeling: I think sometimes it's hard for white American Latter-day Saints to understand what the Spirit of

Elijah can feel like for people from minority cultures. When our hearts turn, they turn with tangible power.

Maybe my friends' disapproval was why I wanted so much to tell Lama that I was going to Israel. Yes, we came from different sides of the political struggle there, but we both really cared about the place. I thought she might be pleased that I would be working on Jewish-Arab cooperative efforts. In my mind, my work in Israel would benefit both of our communities. It might even end up helping someone in her extended family.

That wasn't the way Lama saw things at all. "Why are you doing that?" she asked me instead. The question was really personal. We'd always enjoyed talking together, despite our differences in perspective, and maybe she'd hoped she was changing my mind about Zionism more than she did. She felt betrayed that I would still go to Israel, even knowing how she felt. To her, every additional Jew immigrating to Israel increased the pressure on Arab Israelis and Palestinians. She worried people like me were displacing the people she felt most connected to. Why couldn't we stay in America?

Aaron and David Luna were my main source of BYU support. They were ecstatic: Israel represented so much hope for both of them. David imagined himself happier there and saw getting to Israel as its own accomplishment. I'd put him in touch with Yaakov, the haredi Jew who'd offered me matzah when we met in a park on my mission, and Yaakov had gotten him interested in studying in Israel in a yeshiva specifically meant for the ba'alei teshuva—a Jew curious about returning to Orthodox observance from other faiths or other branches of Judaism.

Aaron was more drawn to the way Israel dramatized Jewish dignity. I remember him telling me to make the most of my announcement. "Don't tell anybody else on the Birthright trip what you're planning," he said. "Wait until the last night, when they're all reflecting on what they've seen, and then make the big announcement to all the Birthright kids. Tell them you won't be getting on the flight back home. Just say, 'Guys, I'm stayin' right here. The exile is over for me.'" He thought the drama of saving the announcement would make the biggest impression on them. Aaron had a real missionary fervor for the Zionist cause.

In June 2007, the big day finally came. I'd packed up the things I would need to start my new life. I'd also thought hard about how to present myself. After I first read the Book of Mormon, I had wanted to live an outwardly Jewish life while integrating my private religious convictions. In the state of Israel, where proselytizing was inappropriate, I intended to do just that. But which type of Jewish life did I want to live?

I decided to wear a kippah, choosing the colorful, knitted kind that signals a religious Zionist rather than the black kippah more popular among the haredim. I also wore tzitzit, the tassels designed to remind an observant male Jew of the commandments. They hang from a sort of undershirt, which I wore over my Latter-day Saint temple garments. I planned to pray and attend religious services with both Jews and Latter-day Saints. Once I started a job search, my clothing would let people know at a glance that I was someone who kept the Sabbath. Both as a Jew and a Latter-day Saint, that was important with me.

With a bunch of other college students on the Birthright trip, I took the flight from New York City to Tel Aviv. Everyone was excited to be leaving home and going out on an adventure. I wonder if any of them also felt the same intense longing beneath the surface vacation atmosphere. The journey meant so much for me: this was my dream, my obsession, since the final months of my mission in Monsey, New York. Now it was coming to pass. When we arrived, my heart was bursting out of my chest.

I was in the land of Abraham, and Isaac, and Jacob. The land, too, of Jesus, who I believed would return as a lion Messiah, fulfilling all the prophecies. Even the air felt charged to me, like Israel had a different spiritual humidity. I thought of the Force from *Star Wars* and how the prequel films said it was manifest in tiny particles in certain people or places. In Israel, that idea of midichlorians finally made sense to me.

Some of that power may have come from the landscape itself. Accompanied by young soldiers from the Israel Defense Forces (IDF), who had been assigned to travel with us to help forge personal bonds between Diaspora and Israeli Jewry, we took time for hikes, reaching up to vantage points where we could see for miles around. The Bible and Jewish prayers alike thank God for the goodliness of the land, for earth that brings forth bread, and for the fruit of the vine. Sometimes, looking out of tour bus windows, it seemed like Israelis had filled every acre with agriculture, making the wilderness blossom as a rose. There's a power in seeing homes and farms and vineyards, hillsides and streams. A power in feeling the wind on your face in this slice of promise between the desert and the sea.

In addition to seeing modern Israel, we took time for historic sites. On the Birthright trip, we visited Jerusalem's Old City and the Jewish quarter. We made our way to the Western Wall. That last wall is like a veil between us and the Shechinah—the presence of God's glory—which still dwells on the site of the old temple. It meant so much to me to press my prayers into the cracks of the wall, like the woman in the gospels who reaches out through the crowd for a chance to touch even the hem of Jesus' garment, or like Latter-day Saint women and men today, writing out the names of the afflicted onto tiny slips for prayer rolls to be placed on our temples' altars. Standing at the wall, I thought again of the Israeli cantors praying toward Jerusalem. Pointing their souls like the magnets in a compass toward a concentration of God.

It wasn't only the ancient Jewish past that moved me, though. I remember visiting the kibbutz where Rachel Bluwstein, who immigrated from Imperial Russia to the land of Israel in 1909, had worked while she wrote some of the first great poetry in modern Hebrew. She had asked to be buried on a hill overlooking the Sea of Galilee. We gathered around her grave while an American Jew who had immigrated told us his story and paid tribute to Rachel's life. I had a lot of appreciation and respect for Latter-day Saint pioneers, but I didn't feel like a pioneer myself when I was in Utah. On the Birthright trip, I felt like I was stepping into Israel's modern pioneer legacy. I could answer Rachel the Poetess's call to be part of this place right now:

> Not nebulous tomorrow, but today: solid, warm, mighty,
> Today materialized in the hand:
> Of this single, short day to drink deep
> Here in our own land.

I could be part of it all. Like the young Israeli soldiers who joined us during the trip, introducing us to what Israel meant to them. Many of them were sabras, people who had been born in the land of Israel. Others had made aliyah themselves. Their faces and features told the story of our people's dispersion and gathering. Some were Mizrahi: Jews whose ancestors had stayed in Israel for centuries, or settled in Bablyon and Persia and remained in those places past the end of the Ottoman Empire, or migrated down the Arabian peninsula and interacted with Muhammad in Medina when Islam emerged as a faith. Others were Sephardi: descendants of the vibrant Jewish community in medieval Spain before it was dispersed to North Africa and the Americas and Turkey and the Netherlands. Still others were Ashkenazi, like me: descendants of Jews who had lived in Germany and Eastern Europe, creating a civilization that stretched across borders and thrived despite persecution for centuries—until its center was abruptly crushed in the Holocaust.

As an American, I stood out as someone with a choice to return to my grandparents' country and expect tolerance. That wasn't a luxury many Jewish Israelis had shared. In Poland, where 90% of Jews were killed during the Holocaust,

anti-Semitic violence *after* the war had convinced many survivors they needed to leave. One IDF soldier in our group was
from a Yemenite Jewish family. Her ancestors had made their
homes in mountain villages at the southern tip of the Arabian
peninsula or in the busy port of Aden. Yemenite Jews wrote in
Arabic as well as Hebrew, using the word *Allah* for God, even
as they traced descent back to specific tribes of Israel: Judah,
Benjamin, Reuben, and Levi. Almost the entire Jewish population of Yemen emigrated to Israel in the late 1940s after attacks that destroyed businesses and homes and killed loved
ones. The few who remained faced periodic anti-Semitic attacks. What did the rest have now to go back to?

I often found myself hiking alongside one of the Ashkenazi
soldiers, named Omri, who had immigrated from Russia. Communist theory had promised a society free from old divisions,
but in practice the Soviet Union had promoted continued suspicion of Jews, especially as part of Stalin's campaign against
his rival Leon Trotsky, who came from a Ukranian-Jewish
family. It had been sometimes forbidden, and always at least
difficult, for Jews to leave the Soviet Union. After the Soviet
Union fell, over a million Jews left Russia and the surrounding
countries, where old anti-Semitic ideas and conspiracy theories still circulated widely. Israel was not only a haven for stigmatized Jews in the 1940s and 1950s: the state of Israel played
a vital role for people like Omri during my own lifetime.

I felt a deep connection to Omri. He looked just like a photo
from my grandparents' house in Chicago of Papa Al in his
World War II Army uniform. The resemblance was so striking
that I wondered if we were distant cousins. In Israel, I didn't
just want to reconnect with Biblical Judaism. I hoped the world
never needed me to be like my grandfather who helped liberate the Nazi concentration camps, but I wanted to carry on a
20th-century legacy of Jews working to defend each other and
find a place in the world. When I hiked beside Omri up to the
hilltop fortress of Masada, where Jewish rebels fell in a siege

by the Romans (and where Israeli military officers accept their commissions today), I swore to myself to do my part not to let the Jewish people be slaughtered and scattered again.

One of our last stops on the Birthright trip was at Yad Vashem, Israel's Holocaust museum, which also houses research into genocide and its prevention. We passed through exhibits marking and memorializing the six million Jewish dead, the homes and communities they built which were destroyed forever by the way Nazis tapped into a latent layer of prejudice and hate. Every Jew still lives in the shadow of the Holocaust. Every Jew's life has been affected by the worlds which no longer exist—and the new worlds the survivors called into existence.

As we walked out of Yad Vashem into an open expanse overlooking the modern city of Jerusalem, we stopped at a memorial with a plaque quoting language from Ezekiel chapter 37:

> *The hand of the Lord was upon me, and carried out in the spirit of the Lord, and set me down in the midst of the valley which was full of bones. Thus said the Lord God unto these bones: Behold, I will cause breath to enter into you, and you shall live.*

For the museum's architects, the roofs of Jerusalem were a fulfillment of prophetic hope: a people resurrected.

On the last night of the Birthright trip, I made my announcement just the way Aaron had suggested. As everyone talked about their memories of the trip, and what it had meant to them, I told them I wouldn't be getting on the return flight with them. I was staying in our land. I was making aliyah.

Aaron had been right. The drama of the moment impressed my peers in the Birthright program. Omri and the other Israeli soldiers who'd spent time with us congratulated me, promising to keep in touch. There was just this huge outpouring of support and admiration for my decision. Living it, though, also felt a little strange. We were encouraged to use Hebrew names, so I used Yehoshua, the Hebrew name I'd been given at my circumcision, with the surname Ben Yona, after my mother. Omri and the other soldiers had decided to call me Yosh for short. And as far as anyone knew, Yosh was a typical American Jew who had grown up in a Reform synagogue. How would these same people have viewed me if they had known I was also a Latter-day Saint? Was I being honest and authentic by withholding that information?

I hadn't mentioned that at all during the trip. I didn't want to betray my rabbi's or the Birthright Foundation's trust by being perceived as trying to make converts or in any way undermining the Jewish identity the trip was designed to promote. The Church itself also prohibited proselytizing within Israel, so not bringing up my layered religious identity was something both groups agreed on. Not everyone will agree with me, but I felt that maintaining both identities was basically honest because both were real. I did want to contribute to the Jewish state as a Jew, did find spiritual meaning praying as a Jew and observing Jewish life rhythms and traditions. I also found meaning in my Latter-day Saint beliefs and identity. Neither identity required the other for legitimacy: both existed on their own terms. I hoped that was enough.

While my peers in the Birthright program headed to the airport, I took a bus down to the new immigrant absorption center in Ra'anana. I remember watching a video there that paid tribute to Yitzhak Rabin, and presented a humanistic vision of Zionism. I remember singing the Israeli national anthem, "Hatikvah," alongside the other new arrivals. Many came from Russia and eastern Europe. Others from South Africa, Australia, the United Kingdom, Canada, and the United States. Two of my new roommates were from Brazil. There was even a group at the center that had just arrived from the Jewish community in Ethiopia.

I could speak English with some of the new arrivals. For others, the modern Hebrew still falling awkwardly off our immigrant tongues was our only shared language.

CHAPTER THIRTEEN

YOSH

◇

From Ra'anana, I began building a new life as an immigrant Israeli. Ra'anana is right in the middle of the Sharon Plain, a green strip of Israel sandwiched between the Samarian Hills and the Mediterranean Sea. It's on the northern end of the urban area around Tel Aviv, Israel's commercial center. There's an industrial park in the town with a lot of tech companies. In that way, Ra'anana feels a little like the northern end of Utah valley.

About one-fifth of the 75,000 people in Ra'anana are immigrants. That's a little high for Israel, but not atypical. The gathering of dispersed Jews to Israel remains an important part of the country's life. Just like in the US, a lot of immigrants arrive in a particular place because they knew someone who knew someone there. Maybe because the city was founded by American immigrants in the 1920s, Ra'anana's immigrants still include a disproportionate number of English speakers. The look and feel of the town was like an American suburb, with wide streets rather than the narrow ancient alleyways of Jaffa or Jerusalem. I could almost have been in Scottsdale, or in Papa Al's Chicago suburb.

The north side of town is more populated by people concerned with Torah observance. There are a lot of modern Orthodox Jews there, religious nationalists who wear knitted, colorful kippot like the one I had chosen. These people believe in building up the state and serving in the military while living religious lives. Not so many were the dark-dressed haredim like some of the communities I'd seen in Monsey, who believed in study over military service and were more skeptical of governments. There was a group of haredim, though, in the nearby town of B'nei Brak.

The south side of Ra'anana is more Reform and secular. It was a lot like home. Some of the rabbis I met would teach and preach in English, even as they prayed in Hebrew. I never noticed any tension in town between the religious and the more secular. There are parts of Israel where those divisions run deep, but here people were more focused on raising families and enjoying a nice, peaceful community together.

Almost everyone in Ra'anana is Jewish. As it grew, Ra'anana came to cover the site of a Palestinian village called Tasbur, whose 2,000 inhabitants were ordered out by the Haganah, the Jewish militia, during the tumult of the 1948 war for independence. Today, Arab Israelis tend to live in large cities or in Arabic-speaking cities and towns closer to the West bank. I lived on the site of one of the many wounds my BYU friend Lama still felt as a Palestinian living in Israel.

I started right away as an intern at The Center for Jewish-Arab Economic Development, which was based in the nearby city of Herzliya. Working at the Center was a great introduction to the country: half the staff were Jewish Israelis and half were Arab Israelis. I wish every new Israeli could work in a place like that, seeing people who come from different histories solve problems together. It was good to work under Jewish and Arab bosses. The Arab bosses were especially warm. Hospitality is a strong Palestinian cultural value and it reached my heart at once.

My position also came with some opportunities to travel

and meet different entrepreneurial Israelis. Wherever we went, we'd meet with various businesspeople to advise them on Arab-owned start-ups and tech incubators they could invest in, which gave me some insight into what both Jewish and Arab Israelis were doing to develop their country economically. Pioneering is an all-in enterprise. It meant a lot to me to soak up the continuing Israeli pioneer spirit, feeling the warmth of energy of people trying to build up the country in a way that could benefit all its inhabitants.

I remember one work trip to Nazareth. I was with a Jewish boss, Daniel, going to survey one of the Arab-owned high-tech businesses we'd invested in. From a job perspective, this was a chance to see an important center of Arab Israeli life. I remember Daniel buying me some baklava, remember chatting with some local people and taking in their warmth and hospitality. At the same time, I remember thinking about how I was in the town Jesus came from. Nazareth's population today is still about one-third Christian, and we walked past some of the historic churches that commemorate events like the angelic Annunciation to Mary that Jesus would be born. I didn't feel like I could stop and linger, though, because of the way I was trying to compartmentalize my identities. I was there as Yosh, a Jewish Zionist. My personal connection to Latter-day Saints' restored Christianity simply wasn't something to bring up in that context.

In addition to work, I also studied modern Hebrew at multiple *ulpanim*, schools for adult education in the language. During the state of Israel's history, this informal network of schools or classes designed to share language and culture has been an important means of meeting the country's huge need to integrate immigrants. . . . I was a little ahead because I studied two semesters of modern Hebrew at BYU before leaving for Israel, but I knew I still had a long way to go. As an American Jew, I'd always felt an affinity for Hebrew in both its Biblical and modern forms. It didn't feel like a foreign language to me, so much as an inheritance that was waiting for me to claim.

Living in Israel made me much more aware of the distance between the way I felt about Hebrew and my practical mastery. In a synagogue or class, you could celebrate every word or phrase you learned to recognize. As an immigrant, I became much more aware of all the things I didn't know how to say. Even as I got better at basic conversation, it became clear just how much language there is in a language! As someone who'd gone to college and read widely, I spoke a lot of English. In theory, I felt I could contribute to Israel intellectually—but the thought of trying to navigate a college class in Hebrew totally overwhelmed me.

In my free time, I would take a look around at different universities. Ideologically, I felt most drawn to Bar Ilan University. Its mission to combine Jewish tradition with secular subjects, fusing together Torah and modernity, appealed to me—and even reminded me of BYU. The language barrier, though, was so daunting. I understand a little bit now how much bravery it takes to stake your future on your ability to make it to the other side of a language learning curve. God bless immigrants everywhere.

Fortunately, Israeli society was very supportive of us. I remember sitting at the outside patio of a local falafel shop, where I ate lunch regularly, when a fourteen-year-old kid from one of the religious nationalist neighborhoods in town sat down next to me to strike up a conversation. He'd noticed that I was an immigrant, but didn't have any negative stereotypes around someone who was learning Hebrew. In his eyes, I was a *halutz*, a Zionist pioneer. Just from seeing the kippah I wore, he also identified me as someone committed to faith in God and to observing his commandments.

My lunchtime friend later insisted on introducing me to his family. His parents were both home when we reached the apartment. "Abba, Imma," he called out. "This is my friend Yosh. He just immigrated from America." He was apparently impressed with my athletic build. "Look at him," he said, showing me off.

"He's so strong. He's going to join the IDF." There's a long history behind that simple comment. In Europe, Jews had spent generations on the margins of society, and often in occupations that required intelligence or dexterity rather than physical power. After the Holocaust, Israeli Jews in particular had worked to project an alternative image of physical strength. Farming and fighting alike were physically demanding pursuits that differed from what many Jews had done while they lived in exile, so both became symbols of the pride of a home. I found out later this boy was active in the B'nei Akiva movement. The group taught ideals of religious piety and working the land, reinforcing the idea of a muscular Judaism.

On Friday nights, I'd often go to different synagogues. I went with my friend's father once. My conversational Hebrew was still so clumsy, but I knew the Hebrew prayers by heart. It was good to speak fluently with God. I also found I felt closer to people I prayed with. There's something we recognized in sharing the same rhythms, the same words carved into our minds and hearts. Religion made me feel more welcome among strangers. At home.

The Birthright Foundation system of having international visitors spend time with local young adults had done its work, too. Omri, the IDF soldier who looked just like a young Papa Al, really did keep in touch with me. We'd connected on the hikes on the Birthright trip and he was rooting for me as I got settled in my new country. Soldiers get the weekend off, so he'd go home and hang out with his old high school friends. He'd invite me down to the beach to hang out with them. "Yosh," he'd say, "I don't want you to be alone this weekend. Let me introduce you to my friends."

A lot of his invitations, though, happened to be at the same time on Saturday as Latter-day Saint church. I'd tell him no, and that I'd come another time, without being about to tell him why.

I understand Israel's caution about the potential burden

of proselytizing. There are over two billion Christians in the world, and nearly as many Muslims. There are about seven million Israeli Jews. Even if only a tiny percent of the Christians and Muslims in the world decided to try to convert Jews in Israel, the place could easily be overwhelmed. As a result, the state of Israel has been cautious about how to protect its Jewish character.[2]

And so, I kept quiet. I lived one public life, and another private one. I am hardly the only person to have struggled to live in two worlds I loved at the same time.

◇ ◻ ◇

The best-known Latter-day Saint landmark in Israel is the BYU Jerusalem Center, a stunning building on the Mount of Olives whose many arches are easy to pick out along the city's skyline. While in Israel, I would sometimes visit the Jerusalem branch at the Center, but that's hardly what my weekly Latter-day Saint worship looked like.

I was a member of the Tel Aviv branch, which met in some rented rooms in an industrial building downtown. Buses don't run on the Sabbath, so I couldn't get there by public trans-

---

2. Debates over Jewish identity are important in Israeli society and law. Israel defines Judaism mostly in terms of birth, as an ethnicity rather than only as a faith, and has no objection to Jews who are openly atheist, or who believe in God but don't see any modern relevance for historical Jewish law. Israeli law, furthermore, extends immigration rights to individuals with even one Jewish grandparent: the same demographic that would have been targeted by the Nazi definitions of who was a Jew. Conversion to another faith, however, is seen by many as a step too far. Looking back, I was in an ironic position. As the child of Jewish and Christian grandparents, I would ordinarily have a claim on Israeli citizenship regardless of my religion or whether I was observing any Jewish customs. As the Jewish son of a Jewish mother, my conversion could be seen as ruling me out of eligibility, even though I was also living a religiously observant Jewish lifestyle at the time.

portation. I couldn't afford a car, motorcycle, or even scooter to drive around, and it was a long bike ride all the way into Tel Aviv. The first time I went to Latter-day Saint services, I'd slept in the building the night before, in my white shirt and tie, because I didn't know anyone and wasn't sure who to ask for a ride. That uncertainty didn't last long. People embraced me and asked about my needs.

There was a family, the Earls, who lived near me, and they were warm and generous with their support. So Friday nights, after visiting a synagogue, I would pedal over to the Earls' home to spend the night. They'd then drive me with them to church the next day. The rooms might not have looked like a worship space at all from the outside, but it's the peaceful, communal feeling in Latter-day Saint worship far more than the physical building I'd felt drawn to.

The branch's members had ended up in Israel for all kinds of different reasons. Some, like the Earls, had come to Israel from countries like the US and the Philippines as guest workers. Others had Israeli family connections through marriage. And a few, like me, were ethnically Jewish and had continued with plans to make aliyah even after embracing the restored gospel.

My closest friend in the branch, Sasha, was a Zionist who had joined the Church in Ukraine (where my own ancestors had lived) before making aliyah. Like me, he was deeply religious, though he'd felt like he needed to work to help his family make ends meet and so hadn't been able to serve a mission. Talking with Sasha was nice because I felt like I could be my full self: a Jew, a Mormon, a young adult. I remember renting a car together and driving around the northern part of Israel, just enjoying the country we'd chosen and having fun together.

I also dated a young woman in the Tel Aviv branch. She was ethnically Armenian, like many of the early members of the Church in the Middle East, but her stepmother was Jewish Israeli. She was really bright, interesting, and accomplished.

She was working at the American embassy as a translator and assistant while doing a master's degree at Hebrew University, studying the Arab-Israeli conflict.

We always had things to talk about. Sometimes, it was the Arab-Israeli conflict, which she thought about from all sorts of different angles. It's easy for young Jewish men, like me and Aaron and David, to focus on the Jewish side of the story and rush to defend our people and faith, without acknowledging our missteps and failings. Securing a future for ourselves, though, has to mean understanding others and balancing many desires. There is no victory so secure as willing cooperation.

Balancing many groups' desires is not easy when they're in such a knot. Jews who gathered to, or fled to, Israel brought different ideas about what the country should be and have adopted different attitudes about their neighbors. Palestinians and Arabs from neighboring countries have likewise brought different frames to the question of what to do about a land with a religiously and ethnically diverse population. And other groups, like Armenians, have a longstanding presence and real stake in this land. My girlfriend had spent a lot of time studying the history of Jerusalem's Armenian quarter. She once took me to meet the Patriarch of the Armenian Apostolic Church in Jerusalem. He struck me as a holy, kind man—like a Jewish rebbe or a Latter-day Saint patriarch, he was someone who represented the connections both between God and man and between the children and their forefathers and foremothers. Faith may divide us, but it also grounds us. Meeting with him, I sensed how faith anchors us to earth even as it orients us heavenward.

How can you help but want peace in a place so rich with meaning? And yet: how can you get peace when there are so many versions of what it should look like? One thing that has made the Israeli-Palestinian conflict so complicated is that there's no consensus on whether the Palestinian cause is an anti-colonial struggle with the aim of Jewish abandonment of

Israel, a theological struggle to keep lands under Islamic rule, or a social struggle for civil rights and quality of life in a state where a regular military presence has become a fact of life. For Jewish Israelis, debates about what society should look like play out on an ice-thin surface above deeper anxieties about whether, in the face of sustained anti-Semitism and violence, their society will continue to exist.

My girlfriend and I didn't only talk about politics, of course. Even when you live in a place where the existential questions are close to the surface of both sides, it's dangerous to let your political questions and ideals choke out the rest of life. We'd also talk about culture: art, literature, music, philosophy, history. We'd appreciate the outdoors, and the ways people settle in alongside the rest of God's creation. I enjoyed going with her to Jaffa, where the old streets are narrow and hand-laid paving stones sometimes stop and make way for palm trees. She'd teach me about all the historical cultures layered over each other in the space around that ancient harbor. She seemed to know all the ins and outs. It was like she'd soaked in this place's past. She took me to plays, concerts, poetry readings. I'd watch her slip seamlessly between fluent English and Hebrew as she guided me through the beauty and wonder of her world.

I may not have known how to reconcile all its parts, but I was making a life for myself in Israel. Omri and his friends welcomed the Zionist in me. My neighbors in Ra'anana showed me hospitality and took me in. In the Tel Aviv branch, I was finding friendship and romance.

After just three months in Israel, I was able to go into an office in the Ministry of Interior to officially have my citizenship application reviewed. The process was surprisingly mundane and bureaucratic. There was no ceremony or celebration. I just waited in a long line, took a number, and was finally called back for an official to examine documents detailing my ancestry. I thought about Grandma Gilda, thought about the soil from Israel in my hands as I stood by her grave. I hoped she was glad I had come here. After the ministry had time to process my application, the official said simply, "Your citizenship has been approved."

There were still some missing pieces left to make the dream really work. The main one, actually, *was* work itself. My internship ended at the same time I got citizenship. I found another position in the area doing data entry for a tech firm, but that was a temporary solution. I knew I needed more education to serve Israeli society and the Jewish people to the best of my potential.

After looking around at more colleges, I decided I just wasn't good enough at Hebrew yet to get what I wanted out of a place like Bar Ilan. Tel Aviv University didn't have any BA programs available in English at the time, either. I'd visited Hebrew University in Jerusalem and loved the way its limestone walls stood out against a backdrop of gentle Judean hills, but couldn't quite figure out where I might fit there. I also wanted to stay close to my girlfriend and close friends in the Tel Aviv branch. When you're in a new country, trying to find your place, every human connection means a little bit more. I wanted to hold on to what I had.

In Herzliya, I visited a much less picturesque campus: the Interdisciplinary Center held classes on a former military base. As a private university, it was more expensive than Israel's public schools—but it had a lot more classes in English. I was worried about how I would pay for it, but applied anyway. If I was accepted, I would find a way to attend. After a few weeks of anxiety, the acceptance letter came. I would even have my pick of programs in government, communications, or computer science.

Everything was coming together.

◇ ◻ ◇

There are some things in life you just count on, without realizing you've done so until they're called into question. Again and again in my life, I've had to step back and get my bearings again after a single experience calls things into question. That happened in the sanctuary when I first met Rabbi Singer. It happened in my backyard when I tried to burn the Book of Mormon. And it happened one evening at a bus stop in Bat Yam.

As a kid, I had counted on the rhythms of Reform Judaism just being part of my life. Because Reform Judaism focused more strongly on Jewish identity than Torah observance or religious worldview, my experiences with my bar mitzvah and Rabbi Singer's Orthodox fervor had called my Reform identity into question. I realized I was looking for something different than what I'd been given.

My startling experience with the Book of Mormon disrupted my life even further. Finding a book outside of Judaism that spoke deeply to my Jewish soul called my basic assumptions into question. I had come to count on my counter-missionary fervor to deliver the spiritual depth I thirsted for. So what did it mean to suddenly find such meaning and promise through the Book of Mormon's presentation of Jesus?

As I embraced the implications of belief in the Book of Mormon, I had come to count on Mormonism and the Latter-day Saint community as a foundational spiritual presence in my life. I had a lot to figure out in terms of how to reconcile the Jewish covenant heritage I'd been born into with my new life, but I could always count on my new faith to place God and his covenants at the center of whatever new shape my life might take.

So it was a real surprise for me, only four years after my baptism, to face the obvious truth that not all active Latter-day Saints shared the same basic aspirations.

I was sitting with my girlfriend at the bus stop outside her apartment, making the most of our time together before I headed back home for the evening. And while we were talking about culture and people and life, she asked casually what kind of wedding I would want, whenever I happened to get married. Since Israel doesn't have a temple, I answered that I would want to go to the nearest one—in Ukraine or Switzerland. The important thing wasn't which one, just that I wanted to be married in the temple.

The answer, which felt like a given to me, seemed to unsettle her. "Why is getting married in the temple such a big deal in the Church?" she said.

I don't know exactly why that seemed to bother her. Maybe it was because only Latter-day Saints who are living the faith's religious and moral standards can go into the temple, and her mother was no longer actively involved in the Church. I understood that could be a concern: my own parents and siblings wouldn't be able to attend the marriage sealing ceremony. But for me, the prospect of a covenant marriage in the temple totally overshadowed any concerns about how the celebration would be different. I couldn't imagine setting that aside.

For her, though, it was hard to imagine setting other things aside for the sake of the temple. That moment helped me realize that religion was a part of her life, but not a foundation. It was a good place to go, a beat in life's rhythm, but not a central commitment she planned to build out from.

That was so different from the way I approached life. My thirst for the sacred had led me into the Church even when it was complicated. It had taken me on a mission, brought me to Israel. I liked her. I admired so much about her, appreciated so much she'd shown me. But it was hard to imagine building a life with her. Not the kind of religious life I wanted, even though we shared the same faith.

Since the Church in Israel was small, breaking up felt like a bigger decision than it might have in Utah or Arizona. I remember sitting in my room, thinking things over and over, and finally working up the nerve to call and tell her I thought we wanted different things. It was hard for me, for her, and for the people around us. Her mother was devastated. The whole Tel Aviv branch seemed disappointed: if two young people in the Church end up together, there's a chance that they'll start a family that can serve as a bedrock of the community. When we split up, that unspoken dream everyone had of another stable piece of the community disappeared. Maybe we'd each stay in Israel: though without a romantic connection to some-one local, many young Latter-day Saints end up leaving tiny branches for another place, or even another faith. It's not like there was an unlimited supply of people to date.

Maybe that, too, was part of why she'd decided that tem-ple marriage wasn't her priority. At BYU, with 30,000 students, it was easy for temple marriage to feel like a norm, like just another step in a good Mormon life. In a place with so few Latter-day Saints around, it was harder to make it one. I can't blame her. Our aspirations get hemmed in by our realities.

What did that mean for me? At that time, temple marriage didn't feel like something I could give up. And I wanted some-one whose desire to marry in the temple felt just as firm. I would rather change my reality than give up that aspiration.

◇ ▢ ◇

Not long after the break-up, I got fantastic news. My friend Aaron would be visiting Israel. David Luna was already there: though he was still an active Latter-day Saint, he had decid-ed to study at the yeshiva that my friend Yaakov had recom-mended. Aaron wasn't sure yet how he wanted to get started with his own stay in Israel, but his visit brought him one step closer. With Aaron in town, I would be able to meet with my Jewish-Mormon Zionist friends in the land we'd longed for.

We met at a cafe in Tel Aviv. Found a quiet table, a little away from other groups of people, where no one would hear our strange conversation, in the mix of references and invent-ed slang that made up our own private language. The setting in Dizengoff Square, a noted shopping district in a cosmopolitan city, was a far cry from Aaron's basement apartment in Provo. But it felt so familiar to all be together again.

I poured out my heart to my friends about the breakup and all my mixed feelings about it. It was a small thing, maybe. David had been through a divorce. The end of a short relationship was nothing in comparison. But he was still sympathetic and supportive. As we talked about the trouble with finding the right Latter-day Saint woman in Israel, Aaron got a thoughtful look on his face. "Why don't you just date an orthodox girl?" he asked.

For a Latter-day Saint, it was a pretty unorthodox question. And in one sense, it flew in the face of my reasoning for breaking up: I wanted a marriage in the temple, didn't I? I longed so deeply for that.

Was it really just the temple, though? Or was the temple a means to an end: a relationship, and a life, built around a rock-solid sacred foundation. Aaron wasn't kidding or bringing up the idea idly. He really felt like the level of commitment to God was more important to a marriage than the particular faith.

The conversation moved on, that thought making little more than an itch in the back of my head. We finished dinner. Then, to celebrate the fact that I had made aliyah, which in Hebrew literally means to "go up," we decided to make an aliyah by going up from the coast to Jerusalem's hills. We'd stand in the city of our ancestors' temple together before we said goodbye.

A week or two later, I found myself sitting on a bus near Bar Ilan University, and noticing a really pretty Orthodox Jewish girl. She was dressed modestly, more modest than you would even find among BYU girls in Provo. And that modesty can have its own kind of allure.

She saw me noticing her. She smiled as our eyes met. We struck up a conversation. Like a lot of Israelis, she had a certain admiration for Americans who were willing to leave the world's wealthiest and most powerful country and make aliyah to the tiny Jewish state. I could tell by glances and giggles as we talked that she was attracted to me, too. Aaron's advice came into my head, then. I started wondering what it would be like to get her number, to go on one date and just play with the idea of a different sort of Israeli life.

She leaned toward me a little when I got up to get off the bus, like she was waiting for me to ask. But I didn't. I couldn't just be the Yosh she thought I was. I had made promises to God. I had found strength through those promises. But I had also made earlier promises to God, and later promises to Grandma Gilda. I thought of her saying I should find a nice Jewish girl and settle down. Could I do that? If God still remembered the house of Israel, as Mormonism taught, what would be wrong with me quietly returning fully to Judaism?

I didn't know. I still couldn't do it. In Mormonism, I'd felt God's presence. In Mormonism, I'd found a modern prophetic voice. The specific faith *did* matter to me: even if God didn't intend conversion for everyone, it was central to the path he'd shown me. I knew what I wanted.

But none of that took away from the poignance of seeing the disappointment in her face through the window of the bus as it drove away.

CHAPTER FOURTEEN

DUAL CITIZEN

◇

That September, I got a message from back home. After a year as a widower, Papa Al wanted to gather the whole family for a cruise. It didn't surprise me that just having us close was the thing that was most important to him, but it was still moving to hear. My journey had been bewildering for everyone. It was good to know there was a strong foundation under all that struggle, and that Papa Al hoped I would be willing to come back from Israel in December to be with everyone.

Around that same time, I'd gone to an event at the Inter-disciplinary Center in Herzliya, where Benjamin "Bibi" Net-anyahu, a former and future prime minister of Israel, spoke about the threat of rocket attacks from Iran. It's easy to feel an urgency, as a young adult in Israel, to contribute to the survival of the state. Sitting close enough to Netanyahu that he could make eye contact when he looked in my direction, I heard him talk about Iranian weapons research as an existen-tial threat. Thinking about what future threats to the Jewish people might look like heightened my sense that we needed to do *something*. I needed to do something.

While I've had serious political differences with Netanyahu,

I respected his personal example of service in the Israel Defense Forces and investment in counter-terrorism efforts. Listening to him, I thought about what technical innovations it might take to protect Israel from evolving rocket threats.

I had heard about an Israeli defense company that worked on the "Arrow," a missile defense system that could address this very security issue. I had a conversation with one of the recruiters of that company. He told me what kind of education I would need to get involved. "Once you finish a degree in Aerospace Engineering, come and work for us."

That wasn't, of course, among the English-language programs I'd been accepted for. And there was no way I would be able to complete a degree like that in Hebrew, though my limited language skills didn't sound like a problem for the actual job. Well? Netanyahu himself had studied in the United States: maybe the best thing for me would be to go back to my native country, to be closer to my widowed grandfather while pursuing the best education I could, and then return to Israel once I was fully prepared to contribute.

My only real hesitation was that I didn't have everything I wanted out of Israel yet. I knew David was going through a difficult period, and I wanted to support him. And I loved the spiritual depth I associated with Israel as a country. Was I ready to leave, even for just a few years?

After some reflection, I decided on a course. I felt like I needed to go back home for Papa Al's gathering of our family. It didn't make financial sense for me to fly back and forth a bunch between the United States and Israel, so I would finish my education in the US before I came back again. In the meantime, though, I wanted to do more with my time in Israel than data entry.

Judaism's high holy days—Rosh Hashanah and Yom Kippur—were approaching. I decided to quit my job and move to Jerusalem, spending the most sacred time of the year with David at Ohr Somayach yeshiva. They said they had space for me and that I could stay for no cost. They understood that I came from a background they saw as wayward, and weren't too concerned about the specifics. Their goal was to receive me as a ba'al t'shuvah, a master of repentance. What they offered was an opportunity to seek God by joining a long tradition of Jewish study and by observance of Jewish law. These were people who believed that keeping the commandments was more than a personal moral protection, but a way to sanctify and heal the fractured creation of the world.

At the yeshiva, I ate, read, and prayed alongside David Luna. We studied Torah according to the havruta system, where you study in pairs, posing questions to each other and sparking insights. It reminded me of what it had felt like to study as a Latter-day Saint missionary, always having an assigned missionary companion to study with and learn from. Along the way, we were aided not only by living teachers but by generations of rabbis who contributed their commentary. It was at Ohr Somayach that I grew to love Rashi, the eleventh century French rabbi whose works have guided countless Jews through Torah and Talmud alike.

I will always remember the Yom Kippur services I attended at Ohr Somayach. Some two thousand haredi Jewish men gathered together. They came fasting. They dressed in white robes. You could feel their devotion as they poured out their hearts. I knew how to recite Hebrew prayers, but they were talking to God. I remembered how I'd felt praying with the cantors, our faces toward Jerusalem. As the Kol Nidre prayers began, releasing us on this Day of Atonement from the vows we had been unable to keep, from all the righteous aspirations that fall flat, I felt like I understood what they had been pointing me toward. It was the kind of worship I felt like the Latter-day Saint temple pointed me toward, a moment when the heaven opens and the veil between God and humanity thins.

There was a moment during that Yom Kippur when I felt like the gates of forgiveness Jews pray for were actually opening, light bursting out into that packed room and shining in men's faces. In Mormonism, I'd been taught we find forgiveness through Christ's Atonement. On that Day of Atonement, I saw men dressed in white tapping straight into that power and experiencing mercy.

In the Book of Mormon, Enos feels the light of forgiveness and asks, "Lord, how is it done?" I believe I witnessed grace through a faith that recognized the heart of repentant worship without ever speaking Christ's name.

◇ ▢ ◇

I still attended Latter-day Saint church though, now in the beautiful Jerusalem Center, where I could look out through the window over the temple mount. It was good to learn from people there, too. To get everything I could out of both worlds. My only regret is that I didn't know any better how to really be fully a Jew among Mormons than I knew how to be a Mormon among Jews. Each Shabbat, I would walk out from the yeshiva wearing a kippah, and then take it off as I approached the Jerusalem Center rather than trying to explain this visual symbol of my worship in another religious language.

The Jerusalem branch was used to people coming and going at far higher volumes than the Tel Aviv branch experienced, but they still find ways to carry on the core Abrahamic tradition of hospitality to the wanderer. People offered me their time, their attention, and glimpses into their lives.

At Thanksgiving, Carolyn Quffa invited members of the branch to come to her home and celebrate the American holiday. She was a Latter-day Saint from Florida, who had fallen in love with a Palestinian Christian man while they were both in college (at Arizona State in my home city of Phoenix, in another of the crossings of paths that have made up my life). They got married and moved around a while before settling in Ramallah in the West Bank. The paths of marriage outside the

temple and religious intermarriage, which I had conscious-
ly avoided, had worked for her. God meets us all on different
paths. Her children had been raised with the benefits of both
their father's Palestinian ethnic identity and her Latter-day
Saint religious identity. I was eager to get to know the Quffas
better as Latter-day Saints who had truly settled in the land.
Not just for work or study, but putting down their roots there.

David decided not to go with me. To him, the Palestinian
territories sounded too much like Iraq. His experiences with the
Arab world were too tied up in violence and mutual suspicion.
He couldn't separate his worst memories from everything else.
The Israeli guards at the checkpoint were confused, too, when
they saw my Israeli ID. What was I doing heading into the West
Bank? The violence and mutual suspicion made it hard for them
to understand why an Israeli Jew would want to visit friends
there.

Admittedly, the posters I saw in Ramallah, celebrating mar-
tyrs in the conflict with Israel, were unsettling to me as a Jew.
My outrage at those who died as suicide bombers interfered
with empathy I might have otherwise had for those killed by
soldiers. Still, I thought about the Book of Mormon story of
Ammon and Lamoni, who come from different traditions about
how to interpret the past and still built a relationship of mutual
admiration and brotherhood. When contrasted with the Nephites of Mormon's day, who took vengeance and abandoned all
restraint, it's clear which path was superior. The book God had
given me pressed me toward transcending very real and deep
rivalries rather than accepting cycles of pride and retribution.

I believe in Jewish Israelis' right to make a life in the land,
and I accept the role of self-defense in Israel's national life. It
was impossible, though, for me to see the Quffas as a threat.
They were my brothers and sisters, fellow children of God.
They offered me their home, their hospitality, their time, their
food. They introduced me to their neighbors, people whose
welcoming warmth felt totally authentic.

Later, at BYU, I would meet (and go on a date with) Carolyn's daughter Besan. She's someone who grew up attending the same Jerusalem Center Latter-day Saint services I did during my time in Jerusalem, but with a totally different experience just physically getting there. She remembered driving to church through a single Israeli checkpoint as a kid in the 1990s. After the intifada, a Palestinian uprising thatbegan in 2000, things got more complicated. To travel the roughly fifteen kilometers to church then often took three hours, with four different buses or shuttle rides between checkpoints with long lines. Sometimes, even with Carolyn's American passport, they would find themselves turned away an hour or two into their journey. To take the sacrament and keep their connection to God alive, they sometimes resorted to sneaking across the border. Besan knew they were risking prison or even being shot, but looking back on her life she had no regrets about that choice. "God watched over me and my mom as we went to church when we could," she later told me. "He knew I needed to feel that spirit that is present so strongly at the Jerusalem Center. He knew that in a conflict-torn place, where there is so much injustice, so much pain, anger and sadness, I could go there and feel peace. I have a testimony that he was looking out for me as I went to church."

That specific testimony became the foundation for her life's spirituality. "I was literally risking everything to feel the spirit, to take the sacrament and renew my covenants," she said. How could I not be moved by her experience and her faith in the face of her sacrifice? It had been so much easier for me to get to Church as an Israeli Jew.

I understand that there is real pain—and rational concern—that separates Israeli Jews and Palestinans. I don't want to pretend the issues that have fueled violence throughout the modern state of Israel's history are things we could resolve just by breaking bread together. At the same time, though, I can't believe that experiences like Besan's are the best we have to offer, or that conflict is the only possible relationship between Jewish Israelis and Palestinians. All the work women and men like my past girlfriend in Tel Aviv have done to study the shape of the conflict is worthwhile if it makes it any easier for us to live alongside each other as our two peoples stumble toward the hope of peace.

I recognize it's not simple. At the time I visited the Quffas, I had my own fears and prejudices about Muslims and Arabs, and especially about Islam. I was in high school on September 11, 2001, and theAl-Qaeda attacks on New York and Washington had made a deep impression on me. What a few people had done was played over and over in my world, while the average person in the Arab world got little attention. I still thought of Iran as an existential threat more than I thought about Iranians as people I could have been friends with. And it helped that the Quffas shared a faith with me.

Still, I was glad I had been invited into Ramallah. I'm glad I took the time to come, grateful for the Church nurturing the kinds of relationships that brought me there. And I hope I'm still getting better at hearing other people's stories and speaking up for them the same way I would speak up for myself.

◇ ▢ ◇

That same fall, before leaving Israel, I found out that Rabbi Berk, one of my Reform rabbis growing up, had made aliyah and was living in Jerusalem. He was at the Shalom Hartman Institute, which promotes Jewish identity and engagement with pluralism. Among other initiatives, the Institute invites North American Muslims to come to Israel to study how Jews understand Judaism and Israel and how Palestinians see their religious and cultural identity.

I arranged to meet up with Rabbi Berk. I was interested in his work. I wanted to reconnect with a figure from my past. On some level, I also felt uneasy about my decision to leave

Israel again for the United States and wanted a chance to work through my feelings with someone who understood.

We didn't talk about my past, or where I was religiously. We did talk at length about my current interest in studying aerospace engineering and working on anti-ballistic missile defense, to protect Israel from rocket attacks that might come from Iran, as well as the Hamas and Hezbollah attacks that regularly disrupted or claimed lives and derailed the larger peace process. I remember him complimenting me on my attentiveness to Israel's needs. He didn't see me as backing away from my commitment to my people, but as seeking different opportunities to contribute. He wasn't my rabbi anymore, but it still comforted me to know I had his implicit blessing.

In January of 2008, I said my goodbyes to David, to Jerusalem, and to Israel. It was hard to leave David. It had meant a lot to both of us to have the time together. We wept. Part of me wanted to stay there and support him as he continued to sort through all he'd been through and choices he'd made, but life pulls in different directions.

As I got on the train to Ben Gurion airport, a kind of heaviness settled on me. I couldn't help but feel that going back to the United States was giving up on my dream of Israel. Who knew when I would really go back? At the same time, I felt like I'd been in motion for years: as a student, on a mission, as a halutz. All of those had taken me away from my family in different ways.

I knew I wanted to be with my family forever. And sometimes forever also means now.

I don't have any particular love for cruises. But it was so good to be together. Grandma Gilda and Papa Al used to have the phrase, "L'Chayim, to Life!" framed on one of their walls. Even at age 85, he still danced like a dapper soldier from the Greatest Generation, a Jewish Captain America. This was his motto as we brought in the New Year:

Enjoy yourself, it's later than you think
Enjoy yourself, while you're still in the pink
The years go by, as quickly as you wink[1]

Dancing alongside him, my brother and sister, my cousins, my parents and aunts and uncles is a memory I treasure. Laughing, moving. Seeing the family my grandparents had created, and paying tribute to them as our own most important pioneers.

◇ ▢ ◇

Neither BYU nor the University of Arizona had Aerospace Engineering programs that could prepare me for a job working on missile defense programs in Israel. As I looked at schools that did, the obvious choice was right in Phoenix, at Arizona State. I even visited ASU's Air Force ROTC director, thinking that some military training might be helpful for me, but he told me I'd have to give up Israeli citizenship to participate and serve. At the time, that felt out of the question for me.

I had forgotten what it felt like to attend one of the nation's top party schools. When I was at the U of A before my mission, I was living in co-ed dorms. One of the women in the room next door made some sexual jokes about me I saw as out of bounds. While the dynamics were different for me as a man than they are for many women, coming back to a similar environment still made me uncomfortable. I looked for a refuge in Institute classes, but the time between them was too long. It was just hard to move from the life I'd known in Israel to the alienation I felt in what was sometimes almost a caricature of the American college scene.

One advantage of being back in the United States was that I could talk on the phone with the friends who had introduced me to the church again. Shea, his cousin Matt, and Dave

1. The lines come from the 1949 song "Enjoy Yourself (It's Later Than You Think) by Herb Magidson and Carl Sigman

Thaxton were all just a state away at BYU. One day, while I was talking with Dave about how things were going, I asked him for advice about how to handle them. He answered with an almost Israeli bluntness: "Transfer back to BYU. Come live by me."

BYU didn't have the same aerospace program, but Dave didn't let me off the hook. He knew what was bothering me, and he knew what he thought I should hear. And it had a certain appeal. At BYU, I could have a modern, English-language education, combined with prayer and purpose. I didn't have to go back all the way to a yeshiva to study scriptures with a friend. I could just get in my little green Chevy S-10 pickup, drive the ten hours back to Provo, and be in a religious environment again.

So that's what I did. Not knowing, once again, how all the pieces of my life would fit together, but trusting the next step forward into the dark. At BYU, I signed up for Latter-day Saint religion classes—and got involved with the local America-Israel Public Affairs Committee (AIPAC) organization, a mostly Jewish pro-Israel lobbying group, as I tried to stay engaged with both parts of myself.

◇ ◇ ◇

My first week back in Provo, I went to church as usual—and then in the evening, went back to an event called ward prayer. Ward prayer isn't a common Latter-day Saint tradition: I've only ever known it at BYU, where a Sunday evening extra gathering gives young Latter-day Saints another chance to connect in a spiritual setting. At BYU, male and female students live in separate buildings within the same apartment complexes, unlike at U of A and ASU. Most activities, however, are mixed-gender, different from the male-only yeshiva. I felt most at home in that egalitarian social space.

Since I was new, they gave me a few minutes to introduce myself to the people I would be living near and worshiping alongside. I mentioned something about where I'd gone on my mission. After not being able to talk about it in Israel, it felt really good just to be able to mention it—let alone to know people might want to talk about what I'd experienced! I also mentioned that I'd just come back from living in Israel. That was part of me. Sharing it was important to me.

That's the night I met Sara Ann Terry. She was from San Antonio, and had made it a priority to come to BYU to study alongside other Latter-day Saints in a religious atmosphere. She asked me about my experiences on my mission and in Israel. Some people are interested in my experiences because they sound kind of unusual and exotic, but there's no depth to their interest. I've watched people's attention drift as soon as I move off the script of their preconceived notions. Sara wasn't like that. She was a really attentive, empathetic listener who seemed to be interested in my experiences as a human, not as a curiosity. I left that first experience wanting to talk with her more.

I decided to ask Sara out, but the first two times I asked, she was busy. I wasn't sure if that meant she wasn't interested or if it really was a schedule issue, so I talked a friend of mine into inviting her and her friends to a hockey game. She came. We talked. Before the game was over, she leaned her head against my shoulder. It was so nice—and such a relief to have a sign she was OK with me trying to be a part of her life.

We started dating, and would talk about all kinds of different things. Her major was human development, and it turned out she was widely interested in how people work. It's an inexhaustible topic. We'd talk about the gospel and the scriptures, too, transitioning seamlessly between the world we see and the deeper world we sense.

This was what Dave Thaxton had called me back to BYU for.

As we got to know each other, it came up that she knew Shea from when he was a missionary! He'd served in her ward. It was good to hear her stories about my friend, good to hear at the same time about her family and what they were like. I got to hear from Shea, too, about Sara. She was the sort of person who makes a difference, and it reassured me to know how involved she'd been in the life of her Texas ward.

The more I fell for her, the more I wondered about what a serious relationship might mean for my plan to return to Israel. Marriage doesn't just involve who you love, it also involves what you each want. What your religious expectations are, where you want to live, the kind of life you want to strive for.

If I ended up with Sara or someone else from BYU, would it be reasonable to expect them to just pick up and live as a halutz in Israel? Carolyn Quffa seemed happy enough about living in Ramallah, but that was a different situation: her husband was Palestinian, so one of them would have ended up an immigrant somewhere. As an American Jew with dual citizenship, my situation was different. Yes, Israel was my dream. But I didn't want my dream to crowd hers out.

I ended up feeling the subject out by floating the prospect of the BYU Jerusalem Center. What if, I mused, I decided to get a PhD and ended up on BYU's faculty someday? What if I—or we—ended up splitting time between the US and Israel someday?

Sara thought that sounded lovely. Some people's goal is to settle down in one place, live a simple family life in a stable suburban setting. Sara was all in, instead, on the idea of living as a kind of academic pioneer. For as long as she could remember having plans of her own, she'd intended to leave her hometown and family to come to BYU to develop herself spiritually and intellectually. When her time at BYU was over, she fully expected to follow the University's motto, "the world is our campus," by finding other places to grow and serve. If I did a PhD, that struck her as adventure far more than sacrifice. If we ended up dividing our time between the US and Israel, so much the better.

Sara was a good person. And she made me a better one. Where I was obsessive, she was attentive and adaptable, less caught up in her own goals and more aware of others. I liked how she noticed people on the margins. I liked how she exemplified the Abrahamic virtue of hospitality, the way she gave her time and energy to help others. I liked watching her mind work. I liked *her*.

And I loved her. More deeply than anyone else I'd known.

Sara's ancestors on her dad's side had joined the church while Joseph Smith was still alive. She had an ancestor the prophet had blessed. Her ancestors on her mom's side were Greek Orthodox, and she'd inherited so much culture and strength from them.

That spring, I took her to a Greek restaurant in Salt Lake we loved. I sang her a love song I'd learned in Greek. And then I knelt down and asked her to marry me. She said yes.

We travelled down closer to her family for the wedding. On a beautiful Texas summer day, we went into the San Antonio temple to be sealed. In the temple, you step out of time. On that day, we were Eve and Adam, leaving the garden together. We were Sarah and Abraham, receiving blessings like the stars and the sand. We were promised all heights and all depths. Promised time, and eternity.

All my life, I'd been looking for something. For the grounding of covenant, for the authority of a prophet, for the presence of God. In the temple that day, it all came together. This was what I wanted. This was what I was looking for. She was what I was looking for.

CHAPTER FIFTEEN

ANOTHER PROMISED LAND

◇

I had come back to BYU without a real academic plan. Before I went to Israel, I'd been studying Hebrew Bible and the Ancient Near East, following up on Rabbi Singer's challenge to know my scriptures in their own language. After Israel at ASU, I'd pivoted to aerospace engineering to take a recruiter up on their job offer and contribute to Israeli society. That program wasn't available at BYU. Neither was anything in Jewish studies: like many Christian institutions, BYU remained far more interested in the distant Jewish past than in the vibrant Jewish present.

Now that I was married, providing for a family moved up my priority list. I absolutely wanted to contribute, but I wanted to do so in a way that would put a roof over our heads. Like many Jews who dipped toes into our people's vast store of legal reasoning, law felt like a straightforward possibility. Sara and I decided it made the most sense, though, for me to finish up my undergraduate studies by wrapping up with what I'd started and decide what to do next for graduate school when the time came to apply.

In the meantime, we were happy to make the most of opportunities that came with a BYU education. We signed up for a New Testament class together, so we could take it as a couple, poring over the scriptures havruta-style. When I found out about a student research team that fulfilled research requests for the Joseph Smith Papers Project, I immediately applied.

The project combined a world-class documentary editing effort with the rare luxury of addressing a major religious founder. Most projects that collect and annotate someone's complete papers deal with political figures, like the early US presidents, who were recognized as major figures in their time. Prophets aren't like presidents. Many have operated on the margins of society, outside of prevailing religious and secular norms alike. The records of ancient Egypt are mostly about Pharaohs: there are no chronicles detailing the lives and religious hopes of the enslaved. We have all sorts of writings from the Roman world—but not about Jesus during his lifetime. Even the Baal Shem Tov, the charismatic eighteenth century rabbi who inspired Hasidic Judaism, left almost no documentary traces.[1] Joseph Smith is just recent enough to have given us a paper trail, allowing the world an indirect glimpse into a prophetic career as it unfolded.

Kay Darowski, who led the Provo-based student support team for the Salt Lake-based project, was interested in giving a variety of students the opportunity to explore the modern roots of our religion by helping fulfill research requests. Some of the research assistants at the time, like Benjamin Park and Christopher Jones, have gone on to great careers in nineteenth-century history. She was happy to bring me on, too, hoping that my experience with the scholarly study of Joseph Smith would give me insights that informed any other work I might do with religious history.

----

1. Although the Baal Shem Tov left almost no writing of his own, his disciples recorded his teachings and his acts.

Shortly after I was hired, Kay also brought on James Gold-berg, an MFA creative writing student with Jewish, Sikh, and Mormon ancestry. Since James's Judaism comes from his father's side rather than his mother's, he doesn't count as Jewish by the traditional definition. But I found out he still fasted on Yom Kippur, kept Passover, and cared about living Jewish culture. He was yet another person I could talk with about what it means to be a Latter-day Saint while also carrying Jewish memory. Though he had relatives who'd lived in Israel, James was different from Aaron and David in that he wasn't driven by any personal Zionist aspirations. He was more interested in how stories, observances, and adaptations had preserved Jewish identity in the Diaspora, and in how Jewish ways of making meaning had added to the broader fabric of the world's life. I don't know how many people live at the intersection of Judaism and Mormonism, but I'm thankful God put some of them into the path of my life.

The research itself was really interesting. The documents people leave behind only give us an oblique angle into their lives, like peering through a door that's open just a crack. What they do help us understand is what people didn't know yet, what it's like to be in the middle of a story. Through the Joseph Smith papers, I got to see Joseph reaching for God and finding his way into different sparks of revelation. I saw his concern for the people around him, his longing to keep the community together even when things seemed to be falling apart.

I remember compiling details about participants in the 1838 conflict that broke out between Mormons and their neighbors in Missouri. Most Latter-day Saints have heard of Missouri governor Lilburn Boggs' extermination order, which led to the violent expulsion of Latter-day Saints from the state that winter. It's remembered as a story of faith in the face of persecution, a story that reflects Latter-day Saints' sense of their contested place in American society. Dealing with period documents, I was able to see how anti-Mormon vigilantes followed patterns white supremacists have followed in other situations: working to disenfranchise an unwanted minority, depicting Mormons as foreign, and so on. I was also fascinated by Mormons' militarism in the face of persecution. I identified with an embattled minority trying to find a way to assert themselves, even if their efforts arguably only escalated the conflict.

One assignment I spent a lot of time on was analysis of patriarchal blessings Joseph Smith's father gave. I love that anyone who joined the early Church, especially those who did so over the objections of their families, could come and get a blessing from Joseph Smith Sr. as if from their own father. These blessings echoed the blessings Jacob gave his sons at the end of Genesis. By linking nineteenth century converts with tribal Israel, the blessings helped build up the sense of peoplehood which helped set Latter-day Saints apart from typical Christian denominations for me, making it feel like a fully realized religion rather than just another Christian church.

One aspect of the blessings is assigning people to a lineage within the Biblical House of Israel. Most Latter-day Saints are identified with Ephraim and Manasseh, tribes they associated with gathering the other ten lost tribes and restoring Israel. A few Latter-day Saints are identified with Judah, though that tribe was associated even early in the faith with Jews. From the beginning, then, there were questions about how living Jews, who had preserved religious memory, would relate to those who embraced Joseph Smith's message of religious restoration.

In the Bible, Ephraim and Judah were often at odds with each other, so there was precedent for the awkwardness I sometimes felt trying to find my place among my fellow Latter-day Saints. On the other hand, Isaiah said that the day would come when the envy and strife between Ephraim and Judah would come to an end. I remember contacting David Luna to tell him about Sara. "You've found a nice Ephraimite girl," he said. "That's good. I hope you're happy together."

Around the time I got married, David came back from

Israel to the United States. He felt like things in his life were coming back together. He moved back close to his children and started to attend church with them and his ex-wife, becoming part of their lives again. Things were looking better.

Until, abruptly, they weren't.

The last email I ever sent David was on February 20, 2010. He'd written me upset about anti-Semitic statements he'd read from a past Latter-day Saint apostle, Bruce R. McConkie.[2] I'd replied by sharing some fragmentary notes of an 1841 Joseph Smith sermon, dealing with Malachi chapter 3 and what the prophet read as a promise to the descendants of Levi.[3] Moments like that, in which Joseph Smith's thought envisioned a sacred Jewish future, felt significant for both of us. They helped counterbalance other moments in the church's history, when other leaders like McConkie and J. Reuben Clark parroted views that seemed more typical of Christian anti-Semitism. I thought David would appreciate it.

I never heard back. The next night, David was up watching his kids at his in-laws' house while his ex-wife was out. When she got home, they got into an argument. Like some veterans who have passed through trauma, David struggled with an intense temper. He ended up attacking her, choking her until she passed out. Thinking he'd killed her (he hadn't), he called the police to confess. Then he drove away and took his own life.

The news of David's death hit me straight in the gut. I felt like I'd lost a part of myself. I'd relied on him as a sounding board and friend as I sorted out my own worries about identity.

---

2. The specific quote that bothered him was this: "Let the spiritually illiterate suppose what they may, it was the Jewish denial and rejection of the Holy One of Israel, whom their fathers worshiped in the beauty of holiness, that has made them a hiss and a byword in all nations and that has taken millions of their fair sons and daughters to untimely graves" (Bruce R. McConkie, *The Millennial Messiah* (Deseret Book, 1982), 224–25).
3. The Joseph Smith Papers, "Discourse, circa 21 March 1841, as Reported by Martha Jane Knowlton Coray," josephsmithpapers.org

I know everyone carries their own burdens and makes their own choices, but I felt like I'd failed him. I wanted to believe there was something more I could have done to be there for him while he was searching for peace, some extra step I could have taken to put him on a different path.

Guilt is easier to carry than pure grief. Guilt allowed me to imagine a world in which my friend wasn't gone.

I had dream after dream where I saw him. In my dreams, I'd remember what had happened, and my mind would explain it in different ways. That he faked his own death. That he had joined the Mossad, the Israeli secret service, and had to take on a new identity. I had dreams he would contact me, to let me know he's still alive. Some days, while going about my business, it would feel for a moment like I'd seen him just around a corner or in my peripheral vision. But he was never there. He was gone. I knew he was gone. He had died consumed by a terrible outburst of the anger that haunted him, having committed a serious sin against a person he cared for. Died trapped in a prison of his own shame. And there was nothing I could do about that.

David always called me "Yosh," until the very end. He refused to let that part of me die. But I let him die.

God alone truly knows us. God alone knows how much our scars shape our choices; God alone knows what is just. I believe in God's justice—and in his mercy. For me and for David and for all of us.

◇ ⬚ ◇

That same year, my senior year of college, I had space in my schedule for some electives. I found out that the Arab-Israeli conflict course, which was only taught every other year, was being offered. I had never taken a political science course, and wasn't sure exactly what to expect, but I thought having lived in Israel and learned a thing or two from my past girlfriend there, from Omri and his fellow soldiers, from my internship and from the Quffas, would make it easier for me to get up to speed. After all the work on archeology and ancient Judaism, I was excited to spend some time in the present.

When I got into the class, I was voracious. I would read everything, required or recommended, trying to understand the issues better. The professor was a trained Arabist with academic experience in Palestinian experience, with specific focus on women's experience. She also developed the theme of indigeneity, helping us understand the relationships a people can develop with land they depend on over an extended period of time.

The course content helped me understand the depth of connection people in Ramallah and Nazareth experienced to their homes. It helped me understand the profound sense of loss families in the village of Tabsur must have felt when they were expelled during the 1948 conflict that led to Israeli independence. At the same time, however, ideas about indigeneity helped explain a lot of what I'd learned within Jewish thought about the relationship between the Torah, the land of Israel, and the agricultural calendar of Israel's holy days.

The relationship between the Jewish people and Israel was woven across the centuries into texts we still turned to. Israel was where the Jerusalem Talmud was compiled in the fifth century. Judah Halevi, an eleventh century Jewish poet who wrote movingly about his longing for Zion, had moved from his birthplace in Spain to join the minority Jewish community that still existed there six centuries later. Isaac Luria, the great Jewish mystic and father of kabbalah, was born in Israel in the sixteenth century and was buried there in Safed. The frame of indigeneity helped me understand Jews' relationship to the land even through centuries when far more Jews lived in the Diaspora than in Israel.

My professor didn't seem to understand that reality. To her, there were clear bad guys and good guys in the Arab-Israeli conflict. Israeli Jews were a colonial force, akin to the apartheid political regime that ruled South Africa from the 1940s until the early 1990s. Never mind Jews' unbroken association with the land. Never mind that fully half the population of Israel is made up of brown Sephardi and Mizrahi Jews for whom various parts of the Arab world had long been home.

I've wondered since if Christian and Muslim religious assumptions have gotten in the way of our historical understanding. Christianity emerged in a time period that was hard on the Jewish people, with two ultimately failed revolts bringing down violent retribution from the Romans. Early Christians (most of whom were Jews who accepted Jesus' messianic claims) explained the tragedy by pointing to Jesus' crucifixion—and the role some Jews played in Jesus' death. In the destruction of the temple and the terrors of war, they saw divine punishment.

Over the centuries, that early reckoning with tragedy hardened into dogma. If Jewish exile was a punishment for assumed collective guilt in Jesus' death, why then would that exile have been incomplete? Why were there consistently still at least some Jews settled in the land of Israel after Jesus' death? Historically, Christians didn't look for signs of Jews living in Israel because wandering, suffering Jews fit better into their theology.

To this day, old theological ideas about the fate of the Jewish people still shape expectations about what has happened. The basic assumption of Jewish absence from the land after Jesus' death is shared by both Christian Zionists, who have tended to view the return of Jews to the land in apocalyptic terms, and by Christian and post-Christian critics of Zionism, who see Jews purely as recent arrivals.

At the time, of course, I didn't have a clear sense of what was happening. All I knew was that our valuable study of Palestinian experience and perspective wasn't complemented by readings on Israeli Jews and their history.

One day, it became clear to me how chilling the effects

of that omission could be. We were discussing rocket attacks by Hamas on civilian targets in Israel. In the discussion, the professor tried to push back against the common framing of Hamas as a terrorist organization. After all, one person's terrorist is often another's freedom fighter. "Are rocket attacks by Hamas against Israel justified?" she asked the class.

I don't know what everyone thought, but with only a Palestinian story and postcolonial critique of Zionism available to them, it was easy for class members to feel like the safe answer was, "Yes." As the discussion progressed, I felt more and more upset. Israelis to me weren't some theoretical concept. They were people I'd walked with, worked with, eaten with, prayed with. I couldn't understand how we could sit around and talk about whether it was an appropriate political tool to target their grocery stores and kindergartens. I couldn't understand how the Israeli town of Sderot, which was founded by Jewish immigrants from Iran and the Kurdish highlands and later became a center for arriving Moroccan Jews, deserved to be treated as a representative of European colonialism. Nor could I understand how continued bloodshed, and the accompanying pressure in Israeli society to crack down on terrorism, was going to actually help Palestinian people living with stifling checkpoints and security measures in places like Ramallah. Not too long ago, I had been ready to devote my career to stopping the very rocket attacks we were discussing. Now, American students with no investment in the conflict and none of the Jewish story were playing at a moral thought experiment with living, breathing stakes.

I didn't know how to give context to all the things that had been said in the semester, even if I was sure something had gone deeply wrong on the way to this debate. Before long, though, I'd had enough. I stood up. "This disgusts me and offends me," I said.

The room suddenly got quiet and uncomfortable, but I didn't know what else to say. I sat down. The version of the story we'd been introduced to contained a lot of truth. I couldn't say it was all lies any more than I could have told Rick Ross that his files about Mormonism were complete fabrications. But whether I could explain it to a skeptical audience or not, I knew there was more to the story and that it was wrong to rush to such harsh judgment. Human affairs are almost never the closed cases people all too often present them to be.

After class, two students took time to privately thank me for having spoken up, however inelegantly. Others may have agreed. Some may have thought I was out of line. Some may have thought I was a complicit, racist Zionist who would fully deserve it if I got hit in a rocket attack.

The clarity that emerged out of that day for me was this: I had given up on my plan to defend Israel from rocket attacks. But maybe learning how to persuasively object to such attacks was as important as learning how to shoot missiles down.

I looked at my options. I talked to Sara. I prayed. And I applied to Brandeis, the Jewish university in the Boston area where I'd dreamed of going when I was a kid, to study the Yishuv (the Jewish settlements in Israel before 1948) and the birth and history of the Jewish state.

I've had some lucky breaks in life, and one of them came when I got in! Sara and I packed up and moved to Boston. The fantastic, diverse ward there, which was plenty used to the academic pioneers always passing through the city, took us in with open arms.

◇ ◻ ◇

At Brandeis, I started my studies working most closely with an Israeli professor named Ilan Troen. He gave me the intellectual foundation to understand Zionism, the Yishuv, and the state of Israel. It remains important to me to defend Zionism and Israel, without any loyalty to a particular Israeli government. Troen and other professors gave me valuable tools to talk about hard issues related to that country's past and present. One of my first courses in the program was on the history of Zionist thought. We covered many strains of approaches, both secular to religious. Troen helped me understand the economics of Israeli settlement and how city planning and agricultural planning evolved. He also helped me to see how no one story could tell us everything we need to know, because the subjective realities of Jewish Israelis and Palestinians are bound together like sides of a coin. It is by listening openly to others that we truly learn to speak.

When I took a class on the Israeli-Palestinian conflict at Brandeis, it was team-taught by a Jewish Israeli professor, Shai Feldman, and a Muslim Palestinian visiting professor, Khalil Shikaki. Feldman's family had lived in what is now Israel since the 1850s. Though he was born in Jerusalem, he'd grown up mostly in the town of Rehovot. Shikaki's family had fled their town of Zarnuqa, on the outskirts of Rehovot, in 1948. He was born a few years later as a refugee in Gaza.

People who approach a conflict often try to get a neutral, objective view of events, but I learned so much more by also getting their subjective lenses. The two had an obvious personal respect for each other and a warm relationship. During the class, I even learned they were working on a book about the Israeli-Palestinian conflict together. They liked my approach as a student and offered me a position on their team as a research assistant. Where possible, the book presented objective facts about the history of the conflict. It went beyond that, however, to show how the same facts took on different meanings in Jewish and Palestinian stories. It was a privilege to have a front-row seat of their work telling parallel narratives in a careful, sympathetic way.

At the same time I was learning more from Dr. Shikaki about Palestinian stories about the conflict, one of my fellow grad students was helping me gain an appreciation for Islam and Islamic cultures. Mostafa Hussein had grown up in Cairo around buildings and ruins that attested to the centuries-long presence of Jews in the city before Israel's independence. He'd developed a curiosity about how the two people's histories intertwined. At Al-Azhar University, a center of Sunni Muslim learning that has operated for over a thousand years, Mostafa chose to study Hebrew literature.

I quickly found that I related to Mostafa on a personal level. Both of us were committed to our families as well as our faiths. We wanted to be good fathers, good husbands, good members of our communities as well as good scholars. I was involved in the life of my Boston ward, fulfilling church callings and caring for the people I was assigned to home teach. Mostafa was actively involved with the local Muslim community and built the rhythms of his life around prayer.

Like me, Mostafa didn't drink, was used to jokes and barbs about polygamy, and was sometimes assumed to be a religious fanatic, given people's preconceived notions about his faith. There's a certain comfort in recognizing overlaps like that. They remind us it's possible to find the same experiences on different paths.

In Islam, Mostafa had learned a love for divine law. More than that, though, he'd felt God's love for all people. I found Mostafa's love for humanity intoxicating. Having had firsthand experience with some of the suspicion and prejudice that could exist between Israeli Jews and their neighbors, I found his acceptance of the humanity of Jewish Israelis particularly inspiring. I had accepted Arabs as cousins already, but I had never really delved into the faith most of them practiced. I wanted to understand the soul of Islam because of Mostafa.

We took a class on the life of the prophet Muhammad together. I was really impressed by a lot of what I learned and had plenty of follow-up questions for Mostafa. In some ways, I probably seemed to him like some of the people I'd taught on my mission. I was looking for light from God. We were having sincere conversations about how the world worked at a deep, spiritual level: with Mostafa, I felt free to work on my ideas about the nature of Messiah, the nature of prophets, the nature of creation, the nature of redemption. For a while, I suspect, he may have hoped that I would see the same light he had and embrace Islam.

That wasn't the relationship I had with Islam, though. I felt my admiration growing along with my understanding, but didn't feel called the way I had through the Book of Mormon. The Latter-day Saint apostle M. Russell Ballard once chided Church members for often failing to recognize the difference between interest in conversion to our Church and curiosity about our Church.[4] Missionary faiths have to strike a delicate balance between welcoming potential converts and respecting people within their own paths.

Mostafa was adept at doing both. I have no doubt that he would have accepted a convert to Islam into full brotherhood in the faith. That he would have been willing to give his time to help share his faith with me or anyone else who wanted to drink it all in. At the same time, Mostafa was clear that he respected the path I was on. He saw that I was committed to living a righteous life, more interested in deeds than in dogma. He may have privately mourned that I didn't accept the full range of Muhammad's revelations, but he also recognized that I lived by revelation that was, at its core, from God.

Imagine interfaith relationships as the proverbial glass half-full. Some Muslims might look at me, and some Latter-day Saints might look at Mostafa, and see how we fell short of their framework of what constitutes a complete package of religious truth. They would see the glass half-empty. Instead of focusing on the ways I might have fallen short of his Muslim framework, however, Mostafa saw that the real, living God was a presence in my life. And who cares if the glass is only half full when what it contains is living water?

---

4. M. Russell Ballard, "Faith, Family, Facts, and Fruits," October 2007 General Conference, lds.org

There's a passage in the Quran's fifth surah that Mostafa showed me. In it, God talks about religious diversity. "To each of you We have ordained a code of law and a way of life," the verse says. "If Allah had willed, He would have made you one community, but His Will is to test you with what He has given each of you. So compete with one another in doing good. To Allah you will all return, then He will inform you of the truth regarding your differences." The verse aligned with what I had concluded as a missionary: that while we have a duty to share what we've experienced, religious diversity is part of God's plan. In his presence, we'll recognize how the truths he gave to all of us fit together. In the meantime, striving to do good works is at the center of what he expects from us, and what we should expect from each other.

In our class on Muhammad, we covered a story that became important in our relationship. In the early days of Islam, the tradition goes, Muhammad advised some of his followers to seek refuge from persecution in Mecca by fleeing to Ethiopia. The ruler there, known as the Negus, was a Christian known for his justice. At one point, the Muslims' persecutors arrived, offered the Negus gifts, and asked that the exiles be handed over. These accusers presented the Muslims' young religion as illegitimate and a threat to society. In response, the Negus asked the Muslim refugees to present their own case. Rather than ask them for gifts, as a king at the time might have done, he asked if they had anything from God. After telling their story, the leader of the exiles shared a surah from the Quran. When the Negus heard it, he wept. The words of the gospels and the words of this new revelation, he attested, came from the same divine source of light.

The Negus did not convert to Islam, but he protected Muslims' religious freedom. Mostafa challenged me to look for opportunities to be a modern-day Negus, promoting Muslim religious freedom in a sometimes hostile American society. I hope I have lived up to that expectation. I'm trying.

I talked recently with Mostafa again, to reflect on those days. It's interesting: I remember things that were simple acts of regular devotion for him, like when he took me to prayers at the Muslim Student Association on Brandeis campus. I remember watching Muslim students from diverse backgrounds washing before prayers. I was really moved by their desire to keep their commandments and purify themselves for each daily encounter with the divine. For his part, Mostafa remembered acts of simple service I did for him and his wife, Basma, that did not stand out to me as any different than the way I treated the Latter-day Saints I was called to home teach. "I will never ever forget the day when I woke you up early in the morning to give Basma and me a ride to the hospital when she was expecting," he wrote. "You told me then that I should not hesitate from calling you at any time, day or night, to help."

Ancient concepts like *covenant* can be hard for modern people to wrap their minds around. For me, though, an important part of what they mean is just this: that we strive to be people who can be counted on.

◇ ◻ ◇

At the same time I was learning to appreciate Islam through my relationship with Mostafa, a Brandeis professor was introducing me to new dimensions of American Jewish identity. In my second year at Brandeis, I got a gig as Jonathan Sarna's teaching assistant for his course on American Judaism. It's interesting: I'd always known the United States had been one of the rare places on earth where Jews had found a reasonably warm and lasting welcome. For me, though, Jewish history had much more to do with Israel, plus the places in the Middle East, Europe, and northern Africa where Jews had moved many centuries ago. We were an old religion, so Ashkenazi Jewish immigrants' passage through Ellis Island felt like a recent blip in a long history of migration.

Sarna helped me see things differently, showing his students—and me—how Jews had been involved in American history from the beginning. We touched on the first individual Jews who came to colonial Virginia and Massachusetts, and the first group of Jews to arrive from Brazil to settle in New Amsterdam. We talked about Freemasonry and the vital role it played for Jews as a place where they could meet with Christians in a spiritual setting as equals, and about how both Christian Masons like George Washington and Jewish Masons like Haym Salomon came together, risking their lives in the revolutionary cause. It was a cause that I found myself feeling a renewed investment in.

We talked about how, in the early 1800s, a distinctly American Jewish identity was forming out of diverse identities Jews brought from the communities they'd come from. We talked about the first major waves of Jewish immigration in the mid-1800s, and how interactions with Jews influenced Abraham Lincoln. By the time Ellis Island opened as an immigration processing center in 1892, Jews had already left an indelible mark on America.

At the same time, America had shaped new sensibilities for many of its Jews. America's great experiment with religious freedom left Jews with more room to think about what it meant to be Jewish and how to conduct religious worship than they'd been used to in Europe, northern Africa, and western Asia. American Jews also found themselves with numerous opportunities to contribute to society through both the arts and the sciences, and had shaped their new country's view of the world. America had not always been good to Jews: white nationalists in America had, for example, succeeded in blocking wider Jewish immigration as the Nazis rose to power in Germany and Europe. Once the United States entered World War II, however, Jewish soldiers like my grandfather had been able to serve in the military and liberate the survivors from Nazi death camps.

The Book of Mormon teaches that the Americas, just as much as Israel, are a promised land. Learning from Dr. Sarna, I began to grasp just how much the United States specifically has been a land of promise for Jews. "The Citizens of the United States of America have a right to applaud themselves for having given to mankind examples of an enlarged and liberal policy: a policy worthy of imitation," President George Washington wrote Jews in Newport, Rhode Island in 1790. "All possess alike liberty of conscience. . . . It is now no more that toleration is spoken of, as if it was by the indulgence of one class of people, that another enjoyed the exercise of their inherent natural rights." For Jews, who had lived as a minority in one nation, kingdom, or empire after another, the aspiration to real religious freedom must have felt sweet on an almost Biblical scale. Washington celebrated that hope. "May the Children of the Stock of Abraham, who dwell in this land, continue to merit and enjoy the good will of the other Inhabitants; while every one shall sit in safety under his own vine and fig tree, and there shall be none to make him afraid."[5]

As Professor Sarna and I got to know each other better, I learned that he saw Latter-day Saints as an important part of America's ongoing story of religious freedom. Jews and Latter-day Saints were both minority groups who had experienced religious disdain and social marginalization. He had a real admiration for the late Truman Madsen as a scholar, a saint, and a conversation partner for Jews in America and Israel alike. Because he was open about expressing that admiration, I trusted he would be willing to accept my Mormonism on its own terms.

Through some of Madsen's work, Sarna was aware of Orson Hyde's apostolic journey to the Mount of Olives and the deep roots of Mormon engagement with Judaism and the holy land.

---

5. George Washington, "To the Hebrew Congregation in Newport, Rhode Island," 18 August 1790, founders.archives.gov

One of Sarna's mentors, Moshe Davis, had pioneered the field of America-Holy Land Studies at the Hebrew University. Given my experience as a Jewish Latter-day Saint, with personal ties to both the United States and Israel, Sarna recommended I focus on that field for my dissertation research. He was particularly interested in American Christian responses to the Six-Day War in 1967.

Academically and personally, I stood at a crossroads. I had come to Brandeis to study with Ilan Troen as an Israel scholar, looking into the country's culture, economics, and politics. My experience with Jonathan Sarna had increased my interest in a religious studies angle, and the way beliefs on both sides of the Atlantic affected the fate of the world's Jews. Instead of spending a research year in Israel, as I'd initially planned to do, I decided to focus on interfaith research at libraries in the United States, trying to understand the relationship between what I was beginning to see as two promised lands.

◇ ◻ ◇

Changing my focus to the relationship between America and Israel didn't mean that I left Israel behind completely. In the summer of 2013, I still went on a short research visit to Israel. My trip started by helping Professor Troen lead an academic tour of the country, designed for professors around the world who would go back and teach courses on Israel and Palestine in their home universities in Canada and China, Argentina and Azerbaijan. In keeping with Troen's interest in the economic and social logistics of how people organized life in the land, we went to the West Bank to visit the Palestinian planned city of Rawabi, designed to attract tech sector jobs to the region. Rawabi reminded me of my work with the Center for Jewish-Arab economic development. It was a reminder that we can only build a more just future brick by brick, business by business and home by home.

After the trip, I stayed in Israel for a few weeks to conduct further research at the National Library of Israel and the Israel state archives. On one of my free weekends, I took a trip up north to Zichron Yaakov to visit my old friend Aaron.

While David and I had rushed to Israel as Latter-day Saints, Aaron's path had led him into a distinct branch of orthodox Judaism in the United States first. He'd visited the Chabad Lubavitch centers in Salt Lake City and in Dallas, Texas. Unlike most orthodox Jews, who tend to establish more self-contained communities, the Lubavitcher dynasty of Hasidic rebbes had launched a program of persistent outreach to non-observant Jews. In New York, you might meet them on a street corner, contacting people like Mormon missionaries, only using "Are you Jewish, by any chance?" as their opening question. Chabad representatives would encourage Jews to pray, to keep a specific commandment like wrapping tefillin, or to otherwise rekindle their desire for observance of the Torah. They would celebrate whatever steps of return to the tradition people were willing to take.

In his longing for the spirit of Sinai, Aaron gradually shifted away from the covenant God re-opened with Joseph Smith at Cumorah. He always retained a respect for the Church of Jesus Christ of Latter-day Saints, but it just stopped mattering to him the same way. He moved into the West Bank, studying for a while at a yeshiva in Itamar, at one of the controversial Israeli settlements in Palestinian territory. While I respected his desire to live a Jewish life in Israel, I wished he'd chosen a different place. From my perspective, Jewish settlements in the West Bank contributed to the challenges Palestinians like Besan had faced.

After his initial experience at Itamar, Aaron had taken the advice he'd once given me, and looked for a Jewish Israeli wife. Through a shidduch, a traditional matchmaker, he'd met Hodaya. They were married and settled back inside Israel, at Zichron Ya'akov in Galilee's wine country.

I arrived on a Friday afternoon to spend a Sabbath with Aaron and Hodaya. We went, as Aaron always did, to his father-in-law's synagogue. Hodaya's family were Iraqi Jews. In the Bible, when the Jews were taken into exile in Babylon (in modern-day Iraq), many simply didn't come back. Jews flourished along the Tigris and Euphrates in antiquity, and the Babylonian Talmud became one of the great repositories of Jewish learning. A century ago, at the end of the First World War, Baghdad's population was one-third Jewish. But while many Jews had stayed in the region through the rise and fall of empires, they didn't make it through twentieth-century nationalism. The harder it got to live in Iraq, the more they found their way to a place of refuge in Israel. A few stayed and experienced intense persecution under Saddam Hussein.

The fingerprints of that Jewish community, though, still surrounded me in the accent members of that Mizrahi synagogue used when they prayed. I could chant the prayers in almost the same rhythm, but we'd each inherited a different sound.

Aaron noticed me praying. "How do you still remember all of these prayers and songs from the Hebrew?" he asked. "It's got to be years for you, right?"

What could I say? You never forget your spiritual native language.

After services, we shared a Sabbath meal back at Aaron and Hodaya's house. Hodaya's hospitality and warmth were fantastic. She knew I was a Latter-day Saint, which also made me a sort of relic from her husband's strange past. She knew he was a ba'al teshuvah, but the specifics of his religious story before he came back to Judaism typically went unspoken. Through me, she was able to get another vantage point on that part of his past and the world he'd come from.

On some level, Hodaya and Aaron hoped I'd join him in a return to observant Judaism. I don't have any problem with that: love expresses itself both in the desire to share a joy you've known with others and in respect if they choose to live within the joy they've found. On a visit to the beach that weekend, Aaron reminisced about the days when we'd shared dreams of Israel in his basement apartment in Provo. He reminded me of my connection to this land and this people, then asked if I'd come back. "We could be neighbors," he said.

I wonder how much he wanted that because it would fit into his Zionist vision and how much he just wanted a friend close again. Knowing each other as we did, we gave each other space to breathe. To talk about what we'd been through with understanding and without judgment. I wasn't going to leave my Latter-day Saint faith, but there would have been nice things about living close to him, sharing Sabbath prayers and Sabbath meals.

I felt comfortable enough around him, still, to ask what could have been a sensitive question. What had been missing for him in Mormonism? What was the spiritual absence he'd most looked to Judaism to fill?

His answer was simple. Mormonism helped make so many mundane, everyday *things* holy. But it never showed him the sacred side of *time* the way the Jewish calendar did.

◇ ▢ ◇

Aaron and Hodaya were still on my mind when I came back to the United States. What is the place for Jews in the world? Five centuries after Jews were expelled from Spain, Aaron had experienced the continuing force of anti-Semitism there. Hodaya's ancestors might have lived in Iraq since the days when Lehi left Jerusalem, only to feel driven out as people gave in to the twentieth-century idolatry of ultra-nationalism.

My own experience had been different. Jews in the United States had reached levels of political and social acceptance that Jews in Iraq and Poland never had. On the other hand, Jews had full legal rights in Germany in the early 1900s, before the rise of the Nazis fanned old embers of anti-Semitism into an inferno. In the religious timeline of generations, a window of acceptance could prove fleeting.

In my studies, Professor Sarna had introduced me to the works of a twentieth century Jewish scholar named Abraham Joshua Heschel. Heschel was from a Hasidic rabbinical family. In his community in Poland, many had expected him to become a rebbe, but Heschel chose to study at the University of Berlin in the 1930s instead. He felt a need to explain Judaism in a way that reached the hearts of others and create a bridge of understanding.

Heschel was living in Germany when the Nazis came to power. In 1938, the Gestapo arrested him and deported him to Poland. The next year, just weeks before the Nazis invaded Poland, the president of Hebrew Union College in Cincinnati, Ohio helped Heschel get out of the country. Heschel's mother and two sisters, without the connections to escape, were murdered in the Holocaust.

By 1945, the German army had been defeated and the Nazis lost their grip on political power. For Heschel, though, the conflict did not end with the war. In the decades that followed, he searched for root causes of what happened. Beneath the surface of a moral and political failure, he perceived an underlying spiritual disease. In keeping with the Jewish tradition of *tikkum olam*, or repairing the world, he felt a moral obligation to find and face the sources of that evil.

Part of what he saw was specific to Jews. Heschel felt strongly that Christian traditions of treating Jews as traitors, and vicariously as murderers of Christ, had laid the foundation for later conspiracy theories and scapegoating. Together with Marc Tanenbaum, a rabbi who had devoted time, energy, and talents to building relationships between faiths, and John Oesterreicher, a Catholic theologian who had converted from Judaism, Heschel engaged in an extended dialogue with the Catholic church about teachings that had contributed to the genocide.

I was fascinated by the work the three men had done to promote a spiritual vision of religious pluralism. I spent time in Cincinnati to study Tanenbaum's papers at the American Jewish Archives. I went to Seton Hall, a Catholic university in New Jersey to study Oesterreicher alongside those who seek to carry on his legacy.

It is no easy task to face faults handed down through generations, or to replace long-standing traditions with better beliefs. But by 1965, having consulted with Jews like Heschel and listened to converts like Oesterreicher, the Catholic Church was prepared to try. In a statement called *Nostra Aetate* (Latin for, "In our time") the Church presented new teachings on their relationships with other faiths, including Islam and Judaism.

Many passages in *Nostra Aetate* should resonate with Latter-day Saints. The Lord's charges against Gentile Christians in Nephi's vision in 2 Nephi 29: 4–5 come to mind. "What thank they the Jews for the Bible which they receive from them?" the Lord asks in that Book of Mormon passage. "Do they remember the travails, and the labors, and the pains of the Jews, and their diligence unto me, in bringing forth salvation unto the Gentiles?" In Nephi's vision, the Lord is incensed with those who cling to the Bible and curse the Jews. "I the Lord have not forgotten my people," the scripture says.

As if in response to those very divine concerns, the Catholic Church's statement acknowledges the role Jews played in their own spiritual history: "The Church, therefore, cannot forget that she received the revelation of the Old Testament through the people with whom God in His inexpressible mercy concluded the Ancient Covenant. Nor can she forget that she draws sustenance from the root of that well-cultivated olive tree onto which have been grafted the wild shoots, the Gentiles." The statement further acknowledges that God, in Book of Mormon terms, has not forgotten his people. "God holds the Jews most dear," the statement says. "He does not repent of the gifts He makes or of the calls He issues."[6]

Heschel's work, however, extended beyond his advocacy on behalf of the Jewish people. In the United States, he saw symptoms of the same spiritual disease he'd seen in Europe. He knew what it felt like to be a Jew as the Nazis came to power in Germany. He saw telling similarities while observing race relations in his new home. What had blinded so many white Americans to the image of God in their black brothers and sisters? Heschel befriended Martin Luther King Jr., recognizing how the movement for civil rights echoed the cries of prophets like Amos and Isaiah.

While I was working on my dissertation research, Sara and I moved our family to San Antonio, where we could be near her parents—and near the rich collection of Protestant periodicals at the Oblate School of Theology. As I thought about the different ways Christians and Jews had come to see each other, Heschel's ideas loomed large in my mind.

My reading of Heschel had started with his book *Israel: An Echo of Eternity*. It was important for my research, because Heschel had written the book just after the Six-Day War. Far from seeing the war as an apocalyptic sign, as some of the Protestant voices I was studying did, Heschel saw the war's aftermath as a spiritual challenge. He exulted in the spiritual craving he saw in the faces of ordinary people around him as they flowed along Jerusalem's streets. He felt the Shekhinah, God's presence, when he visited the temple's western wall. At the same time, he raised his voice in warning to Jewish Israelis. "We do not worship the soil,"[7] he wrote. If pride in the land became a substitute for spiritual life, he felt, the land's promise would go unrealized. He warned specifically against prejudice about Palestinians or indifference to their plights. "You cannot worship God," he warned, "and at the same time look at man as if

---

6. Nostra Aetate, vatican.va

7. Abraham Joshua Heschel, *Israel: Echo of Eternity* (New York: Farrar, Straus, and Giroux, 1969), 120.

he were a horse."[8]

I can still remember the bus stop where I would sit each day on my way to the research library, because it's where I read Heschel's book *The Prophets*. In the book, Heschel describes how the cries of the prophets give us access to God's feelings for humanity. In the scriptures, I had read again and again how prophets spoke out on behalf of the widow and the orphan, the hungry and oppressed. Heschel believed those concerns were rooted in the prophets' access to God's own raw empathy. "To us a single act of injustice—cheating in business, exploitation of the poor—is a slight; to the prophets, a disaster," he wrote. "To us injustice is injurious to the welfare of the people; to the prophets it is a deathblow to existence: to us, an episode; to them, a catastrophe, a threat to the world."[9]

Heschel showed me how the prophets' message called us all to action. Sometimes we treat truth as a possession and fall into the complacency of the rich when we have it. Sometimes we feel it is enough to honor our rituals. Sometimes we reverence our own advertising, and the image we present to the world. But the prophets call us to refocus our attention and energy. "Pagans extol sacred things," he wrote, "the Prophets extol sacred deeds."[10]

Ever since my bar mitzvah, when I read about Korach's rebellion against Moses, I had been searching for the prophetic voice. As a teenager, I had found that voice in Joseph Smith, and in Gordon B. Hinckley. On my mission, I had immersed myself more deeply in the words of the Hebrew prophets. And at a bus stop in San Antonio, Texas, I felt that same voice in the words of Abraham Joshua Heschel.

---

8. Abraham Joshua Heschel, Susannah Heschel, *Moral Grandeur and Spiritual Audacity* (New York: Farrar, Straus, and Giroux, 1997), xvii.

9. Abraham Joshua Heschel, *The Prophets* (New York: HarperCollins, 2001), 4.

10. Abraham Joshua Heschel, *The Earth is the Lord's: The Inner World of the Jew in East Europe* (New York: Farrar, Straus, and Giroux, 1979), 2.

◇ ◻ ◇

In our ward in San Antonio, I was called to teach early morning seminary. I didn't have a lot of experience with seminary specifically, not having wanted to make a habit of sneaking out. I was doing my best to catch up. The beauty and terror of Latter-day Saint service is that no one really cares if you know exactly what you're doing. In God's eyes, we're all bumbling around—what's a tiny mortal difference in our individual degrees of incompetence?

Every weekday morning, I'd sneak out of our apartment—this time to avoid waking up our three-year-old, Camilla, or one-year-old, Abram. In a room at the church, I'd welcome a group of fifteen students between fourteen and eighteen into a study of the Book of Mormon.

I did my best to remember how hard it was to be a teenager. All the temptations and uncertainty and loneliness that can gnaw at you at that time of life, right as you're working to get comfortable in your own skin and find your place in the world. I love that the Church of Jesus Christ of Latter-day Saints calls people like me to spend our evenings preparing and our mornings teaching because I believe people need daily spiritual bread. I believe that we feed a real emotional and spiritual hunger by giving them a chance to engage with big questions and drink in wisdom tested by time.

Those young men and women were so wonderful. They didn't always keep up with their reading at home, or even stay awake through every session of class, but they brought genuine spiritual hunger. They asked about things that mattered to them.

And in them, sometimes, I felt like I could glimpse our future. A future where we live in a land of promise because we live as a people of covenant. Drinking in what God gives us and reaching out with our might, mind, and strength toward all his children in their many kinds of need.

CHAPTER SIXTEEN

SPACE TO BREATHE

◇

Here at our sea-washed, sunset gates shall stand
A mighty woman with a torch, whose flame
Is the imprisoned lightning, and her name
Mother of Exiles. From her beacon-hand
Glows world-wide welcome; her mild eyes command
The air-bridged harbor that twin cities frame.
"Keep, ancient lands, your storied pomp!" cries she
With silent lips. "Give me your tired, your poor,
Your huddled masses yearning to breathe free . . ."
                        —Emma Lazarus, from "The New Colossus"

In December of 2013, I got on a flight from San Antonio back to Boston, to present a paper at a conference held by the Association for Jewish Studies. I had my notes and my laptop. As part of my routine for any flight, I also had that blue paperback copy of the Book of Mormon—just in case God put someone in the seat next to me who needed it.

The man next to me on this particular flight was wearing military camouflage slacks. That made him an Airman; sailors and Marines don't wear their working uniform on a plane. I asked him what he did in the military. He introduced himself and told me he was an Air Force nurse, an officer. He seemed happy to pass the flight in conversation.

I don't typically need any particular spiritual prompting to offer a stranger a copy of the Book of Mormon. I figure the risk of mildly annoying someone is well worth the chance, however small, of changing their life. And I like to talk, so fear of putting myself out there isn't an obstacle.

What I sometimes need is a spiritual prompting to not talk. Not to look for the moment when I can reach for the book in my bag and tell my story. Sometimes I need God's own whisper to get me to sit still and listen.

I listened to this man. He'd been born in the 1970s in the Soviet Union and had grown up accepting the state's official atheism. His ancestry was Jewish, though he wasn't practicing in any way. It was just one of those things that set him apart from the country's mainstream.

As an adult, he'd moved to the United States, eager to experience the land of freedom he'd always been warned against. After arriving from Russia, he enlisted in the Air Force. It gave him a path to citizenship, and he decided to stay.

I loved hearing about his experience as a Russian Jewish immigrant in the American military. His story wasn't through, though. As I asked him about his military experience, he told me about how he'd met an Air Force chaplain who reached out to him and worked with him. Recognizing God in his life had turned things around, and he'd embraced the chaplain's Christianity. I felt God's spirit as I listened to his story.

After he'd told me about his conversion, he asked me about my career goals. I told him how I was finishing a PhD in religious studies but really admired people who served in the military.

He smiled. "You can still join! The pay and benefits are great."

Before I knew what was happening, we were talking about work-life balance and how military life had been for his wife and kids. "You should think about it," he said. "After talking with you, I think you'd make an outstanding chaplain."

I don't know if that conversation made a difference for him, but it certainly changed me. I'd never thought about chaplaincy before. Maybe it's because Latter-day Saints rely on lay clergy: you can love serving in the faith without ever really thinking about it as a career. I'd imagined myself as an engineer, trying to defend my people, or as a professor, trying to understand and explain them. Listening to this stranger on the plane, I felt a strong desire to serve and minister in a more direct, personal way. Maybe it was the missionary in me, or maybe it was all the Heschel I'd been reading, but being there for someone like this man at the time just felt right. As I sat there, I couldn't get the idea of becoming a chaplain out of my head and heart.

As soon as I got off the plane, I called Sara to share the idea with her. We both got down on our knees to pray, and I felt the familiar warmth of confirmation that this would be a good path for me. Sara must have felt something like that, too, because the next thing she said was, "Let's go for it."

I didn't delay. That same day I called Church Military Relations and asked what I needed to do to become a Latter-day Saint military chaplain. The process included interviews with my bishop, stake president, and a General Authority. After I'd made it through all of them, the Church endorsed me for the Navy and the Air Force.

Next, then, I needed to go through their interview process. The Navy was more interested in me, and Sara was more interested in the Navy's coastal locations! I was interviewed by Navy officer recruiters in San Antonio, by the closest chaplain recruiter in Dallas, and finally by a dozen senior Navy chaplains at the Pentagon. A few weeks later, I found out I'd been selected for active duty.

I'd already accepted, and was going through my security clearance, when a final obstacle came to light. Officers in the military aren't allowed to have dual citizenship, and chaplains are officers. If this was really the path I wanted, I'd have to give up my Israeli citizenship.

I was glad, then, that Sara and I had prayed about this job and gotten such a clear answer. I was glad I had studied with Jonathan Sarna, and that I had the Book of Mormon, to help me see America as another promised land. The time I'd spent in Israel meant the world to me, but sometimes we have to let go of the dreams we've had to find the place God wants us.

I filled out a form to renounce my Israeli citizenship. I let go of that dream. And I got ready to start my training.

I was at officer training in Newport, Rhode Island, the last time I got to see Papa Al. Ever since I'd come back to the United States from Israel, I'd made it a priority to go out and visit, driving up to Chicago every time I went to an archive in the Midwest during my PhD work. He was strong and active, but age comes for us all. By the time the military invited him and Uncle Larry to go on an Honor Flight to the capital to honor their World War II service, Papa Al leaned heavily on his brother. "He was clinging to me," Uncle Larry told me later. Papa Al was hospitalized just a few months later and we knew this might be the end.

I was at church, dressed in my Navy khaki uniform, when my mom asked if I could do a video call with him. I found a quiet classroom and got on. As soon as I saw the exhaustion and wear on his face, I started to cry. He meant so much to me. He'd been an active and loving patriarch in our family for all my life, and I didn't know what to do without him.

When Papa saw me in my uniform, though, a new burst of energy came through him. He sat straight up in the hospital bed. "Jason, you keep up the fight, you hear me?" he said. "You keep up the fight."

Hands on my head in blessing couldn't have given me more than that.

When he died, my mom called the military. Though I was in boot camp and wouldn't normally have been able to leave, my superiors decided to treat him like immediate family as my mom described his role in my life. The funeral was the first time I wore my dress blues. Papa Al had a veteran's funeral. His casket was draped in the flag. They played taps and gave him a formal gun salute in farewell. I was moved when the rabbi asked me to say a few words at the graveside. I knew I'd interrupted the religious line my mother had wished for me to pass on, but I was glad to be such a visible symbol of how we had carried on my grandfather's legacy.

As we talked after the graveside service, Uncle Larry opened up to me in a different way than he had before about what it was like for him to serve in the Navy at a time when there was more casual, everyday prejudice against Jews. He could hardly believe that I was now commissioned as an officer. "Ain't that something?" he said.

Ain't it something?

◇ ▢ ◇

I'd grown up with so much admiration for people who served in the American military. That admiration deepened during my time as a chaplain as I got more and more acquainted with the challenges many people in the military wrestle with.

The Biblical prophets say that the measure of a society is how we meet the needs of the widow and the fatherless. In the United States, military service is one place where a lot of people come when they haven't had great support throughout their lives and want something more than what they've known. As a chaplain, some of the people I worked with came from pretty stable family backgrounds. Most, though, didn't have that help. Lots of dads had left physically. Others were really absent emotionally. I heard a lot of stories about parents with drug abuse problems, parents who were neglectful or physically abusive. I heard a lot about grandparents or other relatives who stepped in and did the best they could.

The towns and neighborhoods some of my sailors and Marines came from weren't a lot of help in creating a sense of community. In many cases, friends were a bad enough influence that the Navy felt like a good alternative. School had frequently been a stressful or negative experience. If it takes a village to raise a child, we've let our children down by putting so many other priorities above community relationships.

We turn to God in our desperation. Most often, people called for a chaplain when they felt their lives unraveling. Life is hard at the best of times, and even the path to joy comes with the friction of discomfort, pain, and guilt. Military life can be especially hard. There are high expectations in any system where you know other people's lives might depend on you. It can be hard to handle your own mistakes even when they don't get you in trouble. Discipline, when it comes, can be swift and strict.

The military draws a hard line on drugs, but a lot of people seek an outlet in alcohol. Alcohol, pornography, and fighting or hazing can also serve the same basic function of numbing negative feelings by providing something else to feel. I remember thinking once that as a place to take your guilt, drinking can address the same negative feelings Latter-day Saints channel into the sacrament and Jews channel into prayer. Reflection and atonement, though, can help resolve negative feelings, and help to give them meaning. The beauty of repentance is that it transforms shame into wisdom, sin into experience. Alcohol abuse and other risky behaviors hide shame in a damp, dark place where it only grows.

God is forgiving. On its own, life is not, usually. The kinds of behaviors people seek out to deal with their discomfort, pain, and shame tend to compound those feelings. When we're in pain, it's easier to hurt the people around us. That was true of Marines' relationships with romantic partners, with family, and with their friends. I'd see people caught in a negative feedback loop, where they tried to chase away pain with numbing, and then found themselves isolated and left with little more than their pain. When we embrace self-destructive behaviors, we can enter a rapid spiral toward rock bottom.

People would reach out to me when things were really difficult. Some of them just wanted someone to talk to. To listen and counsel and help them define their own values and expectations as a counter to all the outside pressure. Some people wanted comfort, just a person to sit with. Or the unexpected comfort of hands on their heads in blessing when I explained it. Some wanted even more: some were searching for God. Crisis can drive a person toward God, but in those moments it can be hard to trust that anyone or anything is really going to be there for you. If so many other people in your life have abandoned you, it's hard to feel like even God is going to be different.

Without knowing at first what they were looking for, the first thing I tried to offer the men and women I ministered to was space to breathe. I wanted them to feel safe bringing their whole story, with all its contradictions. The darkness and the light. The aspirations and the anxieties. We are made up of the things we do and the things we've been through, the things we wish for and the things we regret. People in crisis have the same need as anyone else to find their place in their own story, especially when their old stories about their lives are under strain. When I preached, I would tell the story of the Exodus from Egypt a lot, because we all pass through periods of captivity and wandering in the wilderness on our way to the promised land.

That journey can reach a point where it's crushing just to take another step. As a chaplain, I worked with a lot of people who were dealing with different intensities of suicidal thoughts. I was so glad they were willing to talk. Sometimes, simply naming the pain can tame it, at least a little. The chance to speak without judgment or interruption can be its own kind of medicine. Sometimes, I would remember the trauma my friend David Luna had passed through in the years before his suicide and think: this is someone's David. Parents, friends, mentors, or siblings might not be in my office, but the time my path crossed with someone they loved was a sacred trust. As I worked with each suffering person, my priority was to help them find a way, any way, to reconnect with the world around them and find the strength and skills to hold on.

In many life contexts, you work toward an ideal. In a crisis of spirit, ideals can feel like just more weight. The most important thing is just to start somewhere. Any harbor in a storm.

My goal wasn't to teach people a certain set of beliefs, but to help build on whatever they believed to find strength and comfort. If a person didn't think of themselves as spiritual at all, we might work on reconnecting with the five senses. Appreciating the gifts of sight, sounds, smells, tastes, touch. We'd talk about how boring death might turn out to be and how the spark of life was worth fighting for.

Other people, I found, had strong beliefs but might lack the names for them. I remember talking with one woman about what she believed, finding out the way she'd tried to follow an inner voice. I ended up helping her connect with Quaker writings. It's not my religious language, but it felt like something that might resonate with her. Sure enough, she got really excited about it. It was wonderful to watch her discover something, see her respond to learning that there were other people who had felt the same things she did.

It was so good to see people on their own journeys. In Jewish history, conversion has very negative connotations. I think that's because Jews have so often been treated as religious objects rather than being allowed to act as actors in their own stories. Over the centuries, Christians and Muslims often saw their beliefs as more advanced and Jews as backward holdovers who needed to be brought into line. Jesus had never authorized, let alone advocated, coercive conversion, but it's the unfortunate extension of prioritizing the spread of beliefs over serving people.

Objectification is hardly unique to religions. When I worked with Marines, especially, I'd see a lot of problems that grew out of a mindset of objectification. The military should be about defense, but the intensity of face-to-face combat can lead to a mindset of asserting dominance over others. I saw that in hazing behaviors, where low-ranked troops tried to assert dominance over recruits. I'd see it in sexual objectification: I noticed some male Marines would talk about military enemies and women's bodies in similar ways, as objects to conquer. Part of my work as a chaplain was to call that out and model alternatives. My voice might not feel like much, but Jesus taught that the words and actions of a few disciples can have the same effect as the little leaven that makes bread rise. Chaplains have a role in elevating military culture.

As a missionary, I'd never encountered the same extremes of objectification. Sometimes, though, we'd wind up thinking more in terms of numbers than relationships, casting our-selves as the heroes and people as objects to be taught, with their spiritual lives serving as measures of our productivity. There's real danger in a mindset that allows the missionary to be at the center of any conversion story. Conversion cannot be conquest. It needs to be discovery.

That's why I'd felt so violated when I was young and my friend's cousin had cornered me in the garage, alone, and threat-ened me with hell if I didn't accept Jesus. The problem wasn't that he was sharing faith, but the way he was pushing it. I still remember him saying, "Confess him with your mouth, Jason." Almost like I was being hazed. Preaching should never feel like bullying, but it did when it came from a mindset of Christian superiority and supremacy.

Shea, Dave, and Matt had shared religion in the right way. They offered me the Book of Mormon, allowed it to become a part of my story, but never reduced me to an object in stories of their own. I'd talked to Shea once, curious, years after the fact, how much my interest in becoming a Latter-day Saint had been the reason for our relationship. He was kind of surprised by the question. Not at all, he said. If you had remained a Jew, we'd still be friends. He didn't feel like he would have lost something if I'd never converted: he would still count me as a brother, and his faith would have a friend.

And so as a Chaplain I joined people along their journeys, whatever they might be. From the sailor who found her personal faith echoed in Quaker teachings, I learned a new appreciation for George Fox. A mentally ill Marine trying to reconnect with his Jewish roots by little bits and pieces of observance helped me find peace with my own imperfect practice of the traditions I'd been born into. As I invited people to explore their beliefs, many of them would also ask me questions about what I believed and why. My interest in what they believed gave them permission to be interested in what I believed. And we were edified together.

One year, I found myself on a cruiser with four Muslim sailors in a crew of 350. During Ramadan, we docked in Singapore and I got approval from the commanding officer to take the four to a local mosque for prayer. The people there welcomed us so warmly. After nightfall, they broke their fast with us in the basement and we enjoyed a feast of Southeast Asian halal food. Both our Singaporean Muslim hosts and my sailors treated me as a brother. I followed them as they went to pray.

At Brandeis, I had watched Mostafa and other Muslim students praying and had felt respect for their devotion in worship. In Singapore, something more happened. I gained a testimony that their God was my God: I felt it. I bowed down with them and prayed, unafraid to worship my God in their way.

Every human being tastes the bitterness of captivity. Every human being knows how it feels to wander in the wilderness. And every human being is invited to feel our way toward the promises of our shared God.

Another time I was deployed to train at a base in Yuma, Arizona. Desert all around us. And when spring came, bringing with it the Passover, I took the time to contact every Jew in the service in that area. Commanders don't always understand what chaplains are doing, so I had to make my own little speech to convince him to let my people go, to let us drive out through the desert to keep the Passover.

There, in a tiny community center where a few scattered Jews from the nearby communities gathered, the rabbi leading the seder lifted a piece of unleavened bread and broke it. "All who are hungry," she said, "let them come and eat. All who are in need, let them join in this Passover meal with us."

Wherever the journey of my life may take me, I hope I always remember that. I hope I always remember how completely God's invitation is open to each of us.

APPENDICES

GLOSSARY OF
JEWISH TERMS

◇

Abba   The Hebrew term for "father," often used with endearment.

Aggadah   Rabbinic texts that are not focused on legal interpretation, this genre includes folklore, stories, moral teachings, and practical life advice.

Aliyah,   which in Hebrew literally means to "go up," means
"immigrating to Israel" in the context of *The Burning Book*.

Allah   Yemenite Jews wrote in Arabic as well as Hebrew, using
Allah, the word for God, even as they traced descent back to
specific tribes of Israel: Judah, Benjamin, Reuben, and Levi.
Almost the entire Jewish population of Yemen emigrated
to Israel in the late 1940s after attacks that destroyed businesses and homes and killed loved ones.

Ashkenazi   Descendants of Jews who had lived in Germany and
Eastern Europe, creating a civilization that stretched across
borders and thrived despite persecution for centuries—
until its center was abruptly destroyed in the Holocaust.

ba'al teshuva   Hebrew for "master of repentance." These are
secularized Jews desiring to return to Orthodox observance

from other faiths or other branches of Judaism.

bar mitzvah, bat mitzvah　Literally "son" or "daughter" of the commandments. At the age of 13 for boys and 12 or 13 for girls, Jewish youth prepare for months with their rabbi and cantor to read from the Torah publicly for the first time, leading the congregation in prayers and rituals. This is a maturation event, signifying the Jewish youth is volunteering to take upon himself or herself the "yoke" of the Torah's commandments.

bimah　At my Reform synagogue, we displayed both the American and Israeli flags on the *bimah*, which is the podium where the Ark of the Torah is kept and the "pulpit" from which the rabbi addresses the congregation.

B'nei Akiva　A youth organization established in 1929 which became the largest religious Zionist youth movement in the world, it teaches ideals of religious piety and working the land, that emigration to the land of Israel is a central commandment of Judaism, and that the future of the Jewish people is tied to the state of Israel.

Chumash　A printed version of the five books of Moses in book form, including vowels and chanting marks. It is distinguished from the Torah scroll housed in the Ark.

galut　The Hebrew term for "exile." It connotes a detachment, a missing piece, from the experience of Jewishness. The term points toward the redemption that should occur as a result of gathering.

Haftarah　A passage from the prophets, often one that relates to the week's Torah portion.

haggadah　A Jewish text that sets forth the order of the Passover Seder. It helps Jews remember the captivity of their fathers and mothers and redemption through Moses.

Halakhah　The collective body of Jewish laws derived from the written and oral Torah (Talmud).

Halutz　A Jewish Zionist pioneer, or early immigrant to the modern land of Israel.

haredi (plural *haredim*)   Hebrew for "one who trembles" [at the word of God]. These fervently observant, dark-dressed Jews are also known as "ultra-Orthodox," which many see as inaccurate or offensive. What separates them from *modern Orthodox* is their rejection of some customs of modernity, like some forms of secular education, culture, technology, and the status of women.

Hashem   Hebrew for "the name." It is the way many Orthodox Jews refer to God, not wanting to take his name in vain.

Hatikvah   The Israeli national anthem. Adapted from an 1877 poem by Naftali Herz Imber, a Jewish poet from Zolochiv, Ukraine, it reflects the Jewish people's two-thousand-year hope to return to the land of Israel as a free and sovereign nation.

Havdalah   A Jewish religious ceremony that marks the end of Shabbat and the beginning of a new week. The ritual involves lighting a Havdalah candle, blessing a cup of wine (or grape juice), and smelling sweet spices.

havruta   A traditional, rabbinic form of study, usually in a yeshiva, where a pair of peer-students studies a text together, questioning and analyzing one another's ideas, seeking to come to new insights.

Hebrew High   A once-a-week evening program for Jewish youth of high school age, with classes on language, culture, and other religious topics.

Imma   Hebrew word for "mother."

Israel Defense Forces (IDF)   the Israeli military.

kabbalistic   The esoteric method, discipline, and school of thought in Jewish mysticism. It explains the relationship between the infinite God and His mortal, finite creation. Its primary text is the Zohar, a mystical commentary on the five books of Moses.

Kibbutz   Hebrew for "gathering." An intentional communal settlement in modern Israel, traditionally based on agriculture. The first kibbutz was established in 1909 in Degania, near the Sea of Galilee. Kibbutzim (plural of *kibbutz*) began as utopian communities, fusing socialism and Zionism.

Kibbutz Galuyyot   Hebrew for the "ingathering of the exiles." This term references the biblical promise of Deuteronomy 30:1–5, that God would gather the Jewish people to the land of Israel after their scattering. This idea became the core of the modern Zionist movement and Israel's scroll of independence.

Kiddush   Hebrew for "sanctification." It is a blessing recited over wine or grape juice to sanctify the Sabbath or other Jewish holidays.

Kippa (plural *kippot*)   A brimless cap, usually made of cloth, worn by religious Jewish males to fulfill a customary requirement that the head should be covered in reverence for God. Orthodox men typically wear it at all times. Non-Orthodox wear it during prayer, in synagogue, or other rituals.

Kol Nidre   Hebrew for "all vows." This is the declaration recited in synagogue before the start of the evening service of Yom Kippur (the Day of Atonement). It annuls any personal or religious oaths or prohibitions made to God for the next year, to preemptively avoid the sin of breaking vows made to God which cannot be upheld.

Matzah   The unleavened bread Jews eat by commandment during Passover to remind them of the exodus from Egypt.

Midrash (plural *midrashim*)   Jewish tradition says that not all that Moses was taught was written down. Additional details were passed down orally through the Seventy Elders and to the next prophet, Joshua, and down through the generations, from prophet to prophet, and from elder to elder, from rabbi to rabbi. Some of this information was later written in stories called *midrashim*.

Mizrahi   Hebrew for "of the east." After the Roman destruction of Jerusalem in 70 C.E., some Jews stayed in Israel for centuries, or settled in Babylon and Persia and remained in those places past the end of the Ottoman Empire, or migrated down to the Arabian peninsula and interacted with Muhammad in Medina when Islam emerged as a faith. These Middle Eastern Jewish communities are known as Mizrahi.

Nostra aetate In this statement of 28 October 1965, the Catholic Church presented new teachings on their relationships with other faiths, including Islam and Judaism.

Oneg A ritual associated with the Sabbath, when friends and relatives eat, sing, and enjoy time together.

Passover A major Jewish festival occuring on the 15th of the Hebrew month of Nisan. Its Hebrew name is *Pesach*, referring to the paschal lamb offered in the Temple of Jerusalem. It is also known as the Feast of Unleavened Bread, known as *matza*, to remember how the ancient Israelites had no time to bake bread during the Exodus from Egypt.

Rebbe The spiritual leader in a Hasidic Jewish movement, like Chabad. It has the connotation of dynasties and Tzaddikim (or "sainthood").

Rosh Hashanah Hebrew for "head of the year." It occurs in late summer/early autumn, and is a two-day observance that marks the beginning of the civil year. In Jewish tradition, it is the anniversary of God's creation of Adam and Eve. A major tradition is to eat apples with honey, wishing for a sweet new year.

Sabra Hebrew for a cactus-like plant. It refers to a person who was born in the land of Israel. It alludes to the prickly-pear cactus, with a thick skin that conceals a sweet, soft interior. This is likened to native-born Israelis, who are said to have a similar demeanor.

Sephardi Hebrew for "Spaniard." Refers to descendants of the vibrant Jewish community in medieval Spain before it was dispersed to North Africa, the Americas, Turkey, and the Netherlands.

Shabbat Hebrew for "rest." This is the Sabbath, Judaism's day of rest on the seventh day of the week, Saturday. On this day, Jews usually remember the rest God took after creation, the Exodus from Egypt, and the future Messianic Age.

Shacharit   Hebrew for "dawn." It is the morning prayer of Judaism, one of the three daily prayers.

Shekinah   Hebrew for "dwelling." This term denotes the dwelling or settling of the divine presence of God.

Shtetl   Yiddish for "little town." It is a small town with a large Ashkenazi Jewish population, which existed in Central and Eastern Europe before the Holocaust. They were mostly found in areas of the 19th century Pale of Settlement in the Russian Empire, as well as Congress Poland, Austrian Galicia, Romania and Hungary.

Sukkot   Hebrew for "booths." This is a Torah-commanded holiday celebrated for seven days, beginning on the 15th day of the month of Tishrei. It is one of the three pilgrimage festivals, meaning that Jews who were able to do so were commanded to appear at the Temple of Jerusalem.

Tallit   A fringed garment, traditionally worn as a prayer shawl by religious Jews.

Tanakh   A Hebrew acronym for Torah (five books of Moses), Nevi'im (the Prophets), and Ketuvim (the writings), the Hebrew Bible.

Tikkun olam   Hebrew for "repair of the world." It is the thought that Jews bear responsibility not only for their own moral, spiritual, and material welfare, but also for that of humanity at large. In Jewish mysticism, the performance of Torah commandments repairs the fallen sparks of divine light that are trapped in this world. Once the sparks of divine light are released, they can unify with God and heaven, bringing the world closer to a state of redemption.

Torah   The five books of Moses.

Tefillin   A small set of black leather boxes containing scrolls of parchment written with verses of Torah. Post-bar mitzvah boys traditionally wear them during morning prayers in support of a biblical commandment from Deuteronomy 11:18.

Tzitzit   The tassels of a *tallit* (prayer shawl) designed to remind an observant Jewish male of the commandments. They can hang from an undershirt.

Ulpan (plural *ulpanim*)   Schools for adult education in Hebrew language.

Yishuv   Hebrew for "settlement," this term describes the Jewish community in the land of Israel prior to the establishment of the State of Israel in 1948.

Q&A WITH
JASON OLSON

◇

JAMES GOLDBERG: Your story raised questions for many of the people who read early drafts of this manuscript. How do you feel about answering some of those questions more directly for interested readers?

JASON OLSON: I was really encouraged by all the issues people wanted to talk about! If we keep in mind that my responses are my own and don't necessarily reflect the perspectives of all Jews or Latter-day Saints, I think it's great to have a conversation.

TOPIC ONE:
DIVERSITY WITHIN JUDAISM

JG: We had some questions from readers about the diversity within Judaism. Can you tell us a little more about the different groups within the faith?

JO: Absolutely. The first thing for Latter-day Saints to remember is that relatively few religions have a single Church organization playing a central role in how the faith is lived. In

Judaism, religious law has been more important than a specific organization. Most of the diversity of background and belief can be described through the lens of religious law.

How do you interpret the law? If you think about secular laws today, they come from both the words of the law that are written and from the way courts have used them to resolve specific questions. Over time, Jews have looked to different religious authorities over how to interpret law and custom. Many different labels are used to explain which traditions and approaches guide an individual, family, or congregation. We use various terms to distinguish between sources of tradition, but most Jews recognize a broad group of people as *klal yisrael*, the Jewish people.

JG: Let's start, then, with terms like Ashkenazi, Sephardi, and Mizrahi. What do those mean?

JO: Those labels have to do with ancestry. Ashkenazim have ancestors from the Yiddish-speaking communities in Central and Eastern Europe. Sephardim have ancestors from Ladino-speaking communities in Spain and Portugal. Those aren't just ethnic distinctions, though. Both groups shared the same starting texts of Jewish law, but looked to different lines of authorities to interpret them. It's like each had their own Supreme Court. As just one small example of how this plays out: both groups avoid leavened bread on Passover, but Ashkenazi precedent also forbids rice, while Sephardi precedent allows it.

Mizrahim is a more recent term: it describes the descendants of the Jewish communities in places like Iraq, Iran, and Yemen. Mizrahi Jews aren't united by a single body of precedent: each group had their own local traditions and authorities. So you might see a congregation that's made up entirely of Jews who follow Yemeni traditions meeting separately from a group who follows Persian ones.

About nine in ten American Jews come from Ashkenazi backgrounds. In Israel, it's more like four in ten. The majority of

Israeli Jews today are Sephardi or Mizrahi. As a result, the North African and West Asian influences on Judaism are a lot more visible there.

JG: In the book, we also talk about Reform, Conservative, and Orthodox Jews. What are all those terms getting at?

JO: For centuries, the most defining differences between Jewish communities had to do with where they got their religious rulings. Over the past few centuries, as new technologies and cultural developments changed the rhythms of life for people, the philosophical assumptions people brought to law also became important. Terms like Reform, Conservative, and Orthodox describe big picture differences in approach. These are recent labels, dating back only to the late late 1800s. Judaism is a very old religion, but the ways it's lived are constantly evolving and changing.

I grew up in the Reform movement, where the emphasis is on the compatibility between modernity and Judaism. In Reform Judaism, the texts that form the basis of Jewish law are viewed more loosely. All the commandments given at Sinai are not necessarily seen as binding for all generations, perhaps only binding in the generation in which they were given and for the Jews entering the land of Israel in antiquity. The focus tends to be on ethical principles rather than ritual details. Further, Reform Judaism focuses on the Jewish Diaspora as a "light to the nations," which results in Jews giving up some identity boundaries inside non-Jewish nations. Reform congregations have been most willing to make changes and accept innovations from the larger society.

Reform Judaism was also on the forefront of gender integration. In the 19th century, Reform congregations became the first to allow women into historically male prayers and spaces. Since 1972, women have been ordained as rabbis. In a

2016 survey, about one-third of Reform rabbis were women.[1]

Conservative Judaism has also been open to change, but from a different philosophical position. Its view is that Jewish law is binding, but can be interpreted and applied considering modern conditions. This means holding on to the starting texts, but not necessarily to the subsequent centuries of rabbinical rulings. Conservative authorities feel free to reinterpret Jewish law in light of modern conditions, without worrying about whether that's consistent with tradition.

This means, for example, that Conservative authorities accept things like driving on the Sabbath as consistent with religious law even though they don't match older traditions of Sabbath observance. The Conservative movement also accepts women as rabbis, though acceptance came later than in the Reform movement. In practice, Conservative rabbis are typically more closely attuned to the details of observing the commandments, while there is less expectation that members of their congregations do so.

Orthodox Judaism remains invested in both the law and past precedent. The oral law is an important concept here. One way of thinking about rabbinical tradition is that it's never possible to write everything down. People who knew Moses and studied with him might hear and recognize things that a person just studying written laws would miss. Therefore, a human chain of transmission through millennia of rabbinic precedent should be preserved. Usually, Orthodox rabbis and Orthodox lay people are both halachically observant, meaning that they follow Jewish law. This makes Orthodox communities look different than Conservative congregations.[2]

---

1. For further reading, see *The Sacred Calling: Four Decades of Women in the Rabbinate* edited by Rebecca Einstein Schorr and Alysa Mendelson Graf, CCAR Press, 2016.

2. For further reading, see Jonathan D. Sarna, *American Judaism: A History* (Yale University Press, 2019).

JG: You mentioned significant differences between the movements in the way they think about how to observe the Sabbath. Can you give us another example of how people in Orthodox, Conservative, and Reform movements might approach the same issue from different mindsets?

JO: Sure. Let's talk about approaches to eating kosher. In the Torah, Israelites were commanded to avoid meat from certain classes of animals, as well as specific practices like cooking a kid in its mother's milk. Rabbinical rulings over generations resolved specific questions. What happens, for example, when a dish comes into contact with an unclean animal? Some of these rulings were recorded in the Talmud. A Jewish family today might respect both the Torah and Talmud, but there are big differences in how they apply those texts.

For example, in an Orthodox household, a family would keep separate dishes to use for meat and dairy products. These dishes would help them follow traditions and rabbinical rulings about not mixing the two. Following those customs would be an act of worship and religious obedience. Orthodox study would include not only which foods are kosher, but also hypothetical questions about what makes a dish count as a milk dish or a meat dish, how to clean one used on the wrong foods by accident, and so on.

In most Conservative households, there probably aren't two sets of dishes. The family might avoid pork and shellfish, but feel like avoiding the mixing of dairy and meat is not an important observance for them. Even if they choose not to mix milk and meat, they may not feel a need to avoid mixing the dishes that touch those ingredients. If they use the synagogue's kitchen to prepare food, though, a rabbi or other authority might help them keep dairy and meat separate. This combination of observance and flexibility would serve to show respect for traditional dietary law while still allowing individuals to eat at a public restaurant without needing to ask a lot of technical questions.

In a Reform household, people might conclude that eating kosher doesn't have an important moral or spiritual function today and simply focus on something else. Not only would most Reform Jews be fine eating a cheeseburger, they might choose to eat pork and shellfish. Members of the same family, though, might choose to keep kosher during Passover to increase the symbolic meaning of the holiday. The underlying spirit of the law is key. If a rabbi in the Reform movement chose to focus on dietary law in a sermon or discussion, her or his focus would likely be on a broad principle like holiness or connection to ancestors, not on obedience to commandments or detailed questions about observance.

JG: Some readers had questions about the terms haredi and hasidic. What are those?

JO: Within Orthodox Judaism, there are different approaches. For example, the term *Modern Orthodox* describes those who try to take rabbinical precedent and adapt it to modernity. The haredi, sometimes called the ultra-orthodox, try to preserve a pre-modern, pre-Enlightenment way of living as much as possible.

Many haredi Jews in the United States are also hasidic, but those words don't mean the same thing. Hasidic Judaism began in the 1700s as a devotional movement, with charismatic leaders working to bring more emotion and mysticism into the community. Hasidic Jews follow the legal rulings and devotional practices of different dynasties of rebbes that can be traced back in a chain of transmission to a few charismatic leaders in the 1700s.

JG: Any other groups we should talk about?

JO: On the other end of the spectrum from haredi Jews, there are also people who identify as Jewish by ancestry and custom but without any attachment to Jewish law and how it's interpreted. These people are often called secular Jews, or hiloni.

Secular Jews might keep a holiday like Passover at home, or

read Jewish books and visit Jewish museums, without feeling a need to belong to a congregation. Numerically, they make up a major portion of the larger Jewish community.

TOPIC TWO:
JEWISH VIEWS OF THE MESSIAH
AND JESUS AS A MESSIANIC CLAIMANT

JG: You've talked about different approaches to law, but a lot of people are also interested in prophecy. How do different Jewish movements think about the Messiah and the Messianic Age?

JO: That's an important question. Certainly, the idea of redemption is a major theme in Jewish scripture and tradition, but ideas about what kind of redemption we're waiting for and what it might look like can be quite different.

In Reform Judaism, there is little focus on an individual redeemer. Rather, human effort and *tikkun olam*, or repairing the world through acts of righteousness and social justice, eventually brings about the Messianic Age. The emphasis is on progress toward a more peaceful and just world. Some Reform congregations have gone so far as to adjust the prayer book to downplay an individual Messiah's role in redemption. Many Reform Jews, furthermore, do not believe in a literal resurrection of the dead, a frequent feature of the Messianic Age in rabbinical commentary.

Orthodox Jews, on the other hand, still tend to await an individual Messiah, a literal descendant of David, who will redeem the Jewish people at the end of time. The Messiah is to restore the ancient kingdom of David, rebuild the temple, gather in all exiles to the land of Israel, and redeem the world, meaning peace on earth between the Jewish people and all nations. Redemption includes the resurrection of the dead and restoring the earth to a paradisiacal state like the Garden of Eden. Orthodox writings tend to emphasize messianic actions rather than human actions as the source of redemption.

JG: Can you give us a little more information about how the claim that Jesus was the Messiah might look through the lens of Jewish tradition?

JO: I think it's obvious to everyone that the world we live in is not fully redeemed. We don't live in righteousness and peace. The dead have not all risen. Because Jesus failed to usher in the Messianic Age, it's easy to conclude that he was not the Messiah. Jews might appreciate or critique certain aspects of Jesus' teachings and ministry, but there's no teaching in mainstream Jewish tradition about two separate comings of the Messiah, so it doesn't seem like a difficult case. The Messiah is only the Messiah if he accomplished all the prophecies.[3]

Christians are so used to reading the Hebrew Bible as predicting Jesus that they sometimes think that belief in Jesus as the Messiah is the obvious conclusion. It's not. Accepting Jesus as the Messiah takes an additional stretch of faith beyond the most obvious meanings of the texts. You need a separate spiritual witness. I believe Jesus will return and complete the Messiah's work. It would be wrong to expect another person to reach the same conclusion by looking at the Hebrew Bible alone.

Latter-day Saints should understand that. It's important to me to emphasize it, though, because there's been such a long history of Christians treating Jews as stubborn and backward for not accepting Jesus. That attitude has contributed to terrible violence and oppression.

JG: Yes. Throughout your memoir, we get glimpses of that history. I was talking to some friends recently, though, and discovered they had never heard about forced baptisms. What can you say, broadly speaking, about the pressures Jews have faced from Christian-majority cultures and how those affect Jewish responses to missionaries today?

---

3. For further reading see: Gershom Scholem, *The Messianic Idea in Judaism: And Other Essays on Jewish Spirituality* (Schocken, 1995).

JO: Most people today can agree that it's wrong to threaten people over religion. Most of us would also feel uncomfortable with a system where you have to practice the majority religion for access to certain professions, to have legal citizenship, or to hold political offices. But that's exactly what life has been like in many societies! Living as a minority group, Jews have often had fewer rights than people in the majority religion.

In Christian countries, there have been some added complications. Many Christians saw their faith as a replacement for Judaism, and therefore saw Jewish beliefs as a challenge to their worldview. Many also blamed the Jews for Jesus' death, which made it easier to blame Jews for their societies' current problems as well. Some Christians even felt Jewish rejection of Christianity would delay the return of Jesus.

Christian mobs sometimes attacked Jews, justifying their actions by appeal to religion. In some cases, political leaders tried to "unite" their communities by demanding that Jews convert, be killed, or leave. Even in peaceful times, Jews sometimes chose baptism into Christianity to gain better access to restricted professions or for other social opportunities.[4] While Jews' civil rights are now protected by law in most countries, history has made many Jews suspicious about the motives and techniques of Christian who seek converts from the Jewish community.

JG: In *The Burning Book*, we touch on a movement of people who believe in Jesus as the Messiah and also claim a Jewish identity. How do most Jews view Messianic Judaism?

JO: This is a sensitive issue. Messianic Judaism seeks to combine a traditional Jewish lifestyle in Torah commandments with a belief in Jesus as Messiah and Son of God. Furthermore, Messianic Jews often claim to be more Jewish in some sense:

---

4. For further reading, see Benzion Netanyahu, *Toward the Inquisition: Essays on Jewish and Converso History in Late Medieval Spain* (NCROL, 1998).

"completed" or "fulfilled" Jews through their belief in Jesus. The usual reaction is what we saw in the Tovia Singer scene introduced early in *The Burning Book*. Belief in Jesus is a marker that one has left the Jewish fold and entered a different religion, Christianity.[5]

Since Judaism is not a religion that defines itself tightly by other markers of belief, however, it's fraught to mark Messianic Jews as existing outside of Jewish peoplehood. After all, if a person does not need to observe any aspect of Jewish law or believe in the God of Israel to be part of the Jewish people, can belief in Jesus take one outside of the community? Responses vary.

One historical reason why belief in Jesus became such a strong identity marker may date back to the Second Jewish War of 132–136 CE. During that war, the Jewish rebel Simon Bar Kokhba fought Rome and established an independent Jewish state for a short time. Some religious leaders at the time hailed Bar Kokhba as the Messiah.

Perhaps because of this Messianic claim, early Jewish Christians apparently refused to participate in revolt. Some sources of the period indicate Bar Kokhba executed Jewish Christians for their refusal to serve in his army and fight for Jewish survival. Various traditions state that many Jewish Christians fled to Pella (in modern-day Jordan) for safety while most of the Jewish people in the land of Israel fought Rome and suffered a devastating defeat. While later rabbis were nearly unanimous that Bar Kokhba was a false messiah, they interpreted Jewish Christian refusal to participate in Jewish survival as a betrayal of Jewish peoplehood.[6]

---

5. In *Understanding Our Jewish Neighbors*, a forthcoming book from the John A. Widtsoe Foundation, Mark Diamond and Shon Hopkin will discuss Jewish views of Messianic Jewish groups at greater length.

6. See Katherine Jane Wright, *After the Star: The Bar Kokhba Revolt of 132–136 CE and its Significance for Jews, Christians, and Romans* (University of Southampton, 2019), 31–37. See also Natan Sharansky and Gil Troy, "The Un-Jews: The Jewish Attempt to Cancel Israel and Jewish Peoplehood,"

The situation today is different. The modern state of Israel is founded on democratic principles rather than a Messianic claim. Belief in Jesus is now a more personal choice with less overt political consequences. The diversity of Jewish identities has expanded. Is there room for recognizing people's links to Jewish ancestry and memory even if they accept Jesus?

My perspective is that Jewish believers in Jesus can make it easier for other Jews to accept our shared history, memory, and genealogy if we do not claim to be more Jewish and as we overtly recognize that God's covenant with Israel remains in effect for mainstream Jews. Personally, I see myself not as a completed Jew, but as a compromised Jew. One who balances Jewish identity with other beliefs and commitments.

TOPIC THREE:
JUDAISM AND MORMONISM

JG: That balancing act shows up a lot in *The Burning Book*. Some readers had questions about what you saw a need to balance. How do you think, for example, about Jewish law as a Latter-day Saint?

JO: In the four gospels, it is clear Jesus lived a Torah-observant life. He kept the mitzvot perfectly. The teachings of Paul and traditional interpretations of his message, however, have left Christians with a generally negative perception of Torah observance. Latter-day Saints inherited those perceptions. I've had to wrestle with a personal conviction that I have obligations from Sinai and a Church culture where people don't always get that.

Sometimes Latter-day Saints differentiate between a "higher law" of the Gospel and a "lesser law" of the Torah. I think that characterization is incorrect. The principles many Christians think of as the higher law actually come directly from the

Torah. The commandment to love your neighbor as yourself, for example, is first given in Leviticus 19: 17–18.

Another theme that comes up is the caricature of Jewish law as only concerned with picky outward details. It is fair to say that the Torah describes both *outer laws* and *inner laws*. Outer laws are external commandments we observe in society, in our relations with other human beings, in our ritual life. Inner laws are laws of the heart. They relate to how we turn our hearts, situate our hearts, toward God and his commandments. Both strike me as integral to a righteous life. I don't think it's right to dismiss outer law as inherently shallow or to say we don't need outer observances anymore! As a Latter-day Saint, I still believe that God cares about both my conduct and my attitudes.

The real struggle for me doesn't have to do with any of those things. It's more technical: Judaism has long distinguished between Torah law, understood as 613 commandments given to Israel, and Noahide law, understood as seven commandments that apply to all nations.[7] In the New Testament, the apostles rule that Gentile converts should be instructed to keep the Noahide law but not necessarily all the provisions of Torah law. That's only for Gentile converts, though. In the New Testament Church, Jewish Saints still kept the law given at Sinai.

Theologically, I accept that I'm under some obligation as a Jew to live the Torah. As a practical matter, though, full observance doesn't always make sense. Especially as a missionary, I felt like I should eat whatever people prepared. I wasn't necessarily able to keep all the holidays the way I would want. I find meaning in the observances I've kept up and trust in God's grace for the rest.

---

7. For further reading see: David Novak, *Image of the Non-Jew in Judaism: A Historical and Constructive Study of the Noahide Laws* (Liverpool University Press, 2011)

JG: Latter-day Saint baptisms for the dead don't come up much in your story, but there has been some Jewish concern about the practice. We've talked some about the history of forced conversions in the history of Jews living under Christian regimes. Do you feel like that history has influenced the way Jewish groups respond to baptism for the dead?

JO: Absolutely. From a Latter-day Saint perspective, it can be hard to understand what Jewish groups are worried about. Latter-day Saints view genealogical work and temple ordinances as a way to remember and honor the dead. The Church teaches that no spirit will be forced to accept those ordinances, but that Latter-day Saints are under obligation to offer them to all the dead. For Jews, though, it can feel like loved ones aren't being left alone even after they have passed away!

Latter-day Saint genealogical work has benefitted Jews in some ways. In the chaotic conditions in the wake of World War II, for example, some members of the Church in Soviet-occupied eastern Germany took personal risks to save books of Jewish genealogy.[8] Latter-day Saint volunteers around the world subsequently digitized and indexed records that can help Jews trace their families.

In the 1990s, however, a Jewish genealogist working with Latter-day Saint sources noticed that many baptisms for the dead had been performed from memorial books listing people killed in the Holocaust. Given the strong emotions associated with the Holocaust and the history of forced baptisms, many Jewish groups expressed concerns.

In response, Church leaders have repeatedly instructed members not to perform temple work for Jews who are not in their own families. Member compliance has not been perfect, but the Church had made an ongoing effort to be sensitive in

8. See Raymond Kuehne, *Mormons as Citizens of a Communist State: A Documentary History of the Church of Jesus Christ of Latter-day Saints in East Germany, 1945–1990.*

interfaith relations.

Limiting ordinances is also consistent with the spirit of Latter-day Saint proxy temple work. After all, the purpose of temple work for the dead has more to do with family than with religious conversion. The goal is to link families through the sealing ordinance, which is unique to the Latter-day Saint tradition. Baptism is most significant as a preparatory ritual for those family sealings.

In general, Latter-day Saints serve best when they focus on ordinances for their own families and leave other ordinances to be done within families. For their part, Jews may feel uncomfortable with the concept of baptism for the dead but can recognize that performing sealing ordinances on behalf of the dead is one way Latter-day Saints with Jewish ancestors can show love and respect for, and longing for connection with, their families.[9]

JG: In the memoir, you mention a few times that becoming a Latter-day Saint felt quite different to you than if you'd become a Protestant. What do you mean when you say that Mormonism found something missing in both Judaism and mainstream Christianity?

JO: Simply stated: Christianity recognized Jesus. Judaism retained temple and covenant. Mormonism felt to me like a beautiful synthesis: a restoration of Abrahamic religion in a modern context.

Belief in Jesus has been immensely important to me. I didn't have that in Judaism. I'm not convinced, though, that belief in Jesus alone would be enough without the concepts that give Jesus' role context and meaning. I think Christians were right

---

9. For further reading see: Elder D. Todd Christofferson, "Religious Freedom Allows Both Mormons and Jews to Honor Their Ancestors," *Church Newsroom*, 10 November 2008; https://newsroom.churchofjesuschrist. org/article/religious-freedom-allows-both-mormons-and-jews-to-honor-their-ancestors

about Jesus as the central figure in God's relationship with us. I think Jews have done better at understanding many aspects of that relationship.

Take the temple as an example. The apostles and other early Christians regularly worshiped in the temple, but after the Romans destroyed it in 70 CE, Christian tradition began to distance itself from the temple. Many Christians came to see the temple as part of an old, unnecessary Jewish order of things that had been replaced by something better. Many Christians have de-emphasized other concepts, like the covenant between God and his people, to focus narrowly on an individual relationship with Jesus.

I think that's a serious loss. If you only believe in Jesus, then it's easier for anyone saying "Lord, Lord," to tell you what else to believe.

Belief in Jesus as the Messiah is not enough. In fact, it is not a teaching of the Torah that belief in a correct Messiah is necessary for salvation. Rather, the Torah teaches that faithfulness to the covenant through obedience to the commandments is the requirement of God. That basic reality gives purpose to Jesus' transformative power and meaning to his atoning sacrifice.

In Mormonism, I could see covenant in Church teachings, in the way many Latter-day Saints treated each other, and in the way they saw their relationship to sacred history. I was able to prepare myself for temple ordinances and experiences. I wasn't asked to exchange Jewish concepts for Christian ones, but to experience the old Abrahamic themes in novel ways.

I also liked how Mormonism synthesized the miraculous with the modern. We don't think enough about the expression *modern prophet*. I've described how there are major divisions within Judaism over how to continue tradition in light of modernity. Latter-day Saints seem to enjoy both the benefits of the modern and the deep spirituality we often associate with pre-modern life. We embrace modernity as a blessing of God, and we embrace prophecy, an ancient mode of revelation and medium for covenant, as something we hold onto for dear life.

TOPIC FOUR
THE STATE OF ISRAEL

JG: We got a lot of questions from readers about the modern state of Israel. You mention events like Orson Hyde's journey to Jerusalem in the book, but could you give us a little more detail on the relationship between Latter-day Saints and the state of Israel?

JO: Of course!

Modern Zionism really took off after the establishment of the World Zionist Congress in 1897. So for Orson Hyde to visit Jews in Europe in 1840–1841 on his way to dedicate the land of Israel for their return is quite extraordinary.[10] At the same time, it makes sense. Latter-day Saints insist that God continues to honor his covenant with the house of Israel, including the Jewish people, and that covenant included a relationship with the land.

There are also interesting parallels between Mormonism and Zionism. Mormons gathered to their own promised land with their own dreams of building up a better society. The Church was involved in extended efforts to promote and organize immigration by members of the faith. Both Mormon and Zionist pioneers felt a sense of sacred obligation to the place they were settling and worked to help the wilderness blossom as the rose. Some early Zionist leaders were aware of parallels. The early Zionist leader Ze'ev Jabotinsky, for example, corresponded with John A. Widtsoe of the Quorum of the Twelve

10. See Jason M. Olson, "'The Kingdom Restored to Israel': Mormon Apostle Orson Hyde's Reflections on Judaism," in Mark A. Raider and Gary Phillip Zola, eds, *New Perspectives in American Jewish History: A Documentary Tribute to Jonathan D. Sarna* (Waltham: Brandeis University Press, 2021), chapter 4.

apostles about irrigation.

Having grown up with Israelis around me, it's not surprising that I have deep affection for Israel. I've met a lot of Latter-day Saints without Jewish ancestry, though, who also feel a certain historical affinity for the country. There are multiple spiritual and historical reasons why so many BYU students, for example, might feel drawn to Israel.

JG: We're now almost two centuries away from Orson Hyde's visit to Jerusalem. Today, there can be a disconnect between religious frames for thinking about gathering and the political issues people associate with Israel. We're less likely to hear about Jewish gathering in Church and more likely to hear about Israel on the news.

Some early readers had strong opinions about Israeli-Palestinian conflicts. Others felt like they should have opinions, but weren't sure what to think. Let's start with a basic question: do you think Latter-day Saints should support Israelis or Palestinians?

JO: I hope they support both.

Looking to Joseph Smith and Abraham Joshua Heschel, Latter-day Saints should embrace the humanity and divine potential in both Jewish and Palestinian peoples. Both have beautiful cultures everyone can learn from. Both have real worries and grievances. Most importantly, both are children of our Heavenly Father.

If you support everything done by the Israeli government or by militant Israelis outside the government, you are probably missing some important perspectives. If you justify everything done by elected leaders in the West Bank and Gaza and by individual militant Palestinians, you are probably missing some important perspectives.

JG: Let's talk about each of those cases individually. I've had some conversations with people who see themselves as staunchly pro-Israel and can be dismissive of Palestinian struggles. What would you say to someone like that?

JO: I am thankful for people who recognize the value of having a Jewish state. Israel has been important as a refuge for Jews who left many different countries. At the same time, I can recognize the impact on other people. Palestinians also have homes and histories in the land. They also deserve to live with dignity.

Sometimes in the US, we tend to see Israeli-Palestinian conflicts through the lens of religion or nationalism, but a lot of the problems are much more mundane. Palestinians who are just trying to live their lives feel the impacts of Israeli policies. For example, water rights are a serious issue. In the West Bank, competition with Israeli settlements has meant that Palestinian communities don't always get access to the water they need. As another example: there's more employment in Israel than in the West Bank, but security checks can make something as simple as a commute to work into a long, frustrating, and frightening process.

You can sympathize with Israel's security challenges and also recognize the challenges Palestinians face. You can sympathize with Palestians who are Israeli citizens and living as an ethnic minority within Israel's borders. You can sympathize with those living in the West Bank, where there are Israeli settlements and soldiers, and with those in Gaza, where there are no longer Israeli settlements but Israeli sanctions and military actions still affect everyday life. The way things are now is not the way we should want them to be.

Many Palestinians wish for an independent Palestinian state as a way to live with greater dignity. As someone who values Israel's psychological role for Jews, I am sympathetic to that aspiration. Some Palestinians have felt the need to use violence in their pursuit of an independent state. That's harder to accept, but I still think we need to be careful about how we assess that violence.

To me, fighting for national independence can be legitimate. I do not condemn every Palestinian action. However, violence for the sake of terror or to drive out an entire population is not legitimate. In other words, I do my best to sympathize when people fight for Palestine but not when they fight to destroy Israel. I feel that it's important to ask which objective any given organization is claiming.

Personally, I hope I live to see a stable and prosperous Palestine as Israel's neighbor. That's going to require both Palestinian and Israeli leaders to make some difficult compromises. One way to support Israel is to notice and celebrate compromises that might lead toward peace.

JG: My sense is that most American Latter-day Saints identify as pro-Israel, and those are good reminders for them. Humans tend to feel drawn for conflict: I love the idea of proactively celebrating steps toward peace.

We also had some readers, though, who see the political situation through the lens of Palestinian suffering and are more critical of Israel, especially when peace feels far away. What would you say to them?

JO: I have no problem with someone critiquing Israel's policies or any given regime. During my lifetime, there have been times when it felt like Israeli and Palestinian leaders were making great strides toward peace and other times when leaders seemed to be making things actively worse.

Sometimes it's hard to watch. Both Israeli and Palestinian leaders are vying for influence within their own communities at the same time they are in dialogue with each other. An Israeli politician might see political advantage in stirring up conflict and do something controversial, like visiting the temple mount. Palestinian leaders might see political advantage in stirring up conflict and do something like encouraging people to rise up, or else firing off rocket attacks. And typically, conflict escalates.

How do observers respond? One option is to place blame on one side. For some people, it's easiest to blame the side with the most power. After all, people on both sides suffer, but Israel's greater wealth, stability, and security mean that Palestinians suffer more. Some people see tragic images or headlines about Palestinian suffering and conclude that Israel needs to fix things.

But Israel can't make peace alone. If you are committed to peace between Palestinians and Israel, you need to look at the entire system. In the 1990s, Israeli and Palestinian leaders took difficult steps toward peace. Those steps involved risks for both sides. Since 2006–2007, when Hamas won elections in the Gaza strip and then executed their political rivals, it's been harder for anyone to summon the combination of trust, courage, and political will it takes to make major compromises. No amount of sympathy for Palestinian suffering can close the gap: Hamas still calls for the entire destruction of the state of Israel, endorses terrorist violence, and renounces past peace agreements. How reasonable is it to expect leaders to negotiate hard compromises under those conditions? How are they supposed to convince voters that it's worth it to try?

You don't have to like Israel's leaders. But you should recognize that they're in a really difficult position. No unilateral concession on Israel's part would be dramatic enough to resolve this conflict.

JG: That's going to be a tough answer for some people. We tend to want quick, actionable solutions to things. Slow and difficult mutual compromise is a hard sell.

With peace between the state of Israel and Palestinian authorities in the West Bank and Gaza so elusive, it feels to me like a growing minority of overseas observers seem ready to give up. I'm hearing more people questioning whether Israel should even exist. What would you say to someone who feels like Israel is basically a surviving vestige of colonialism and that the whole land rightfully belongs to Palestinians?

JO: From a scholarly perspective, I don't think the settler-colonial model is a good fit for Israel. The land has certainly been impacted by the rule of different empires, most recently the Ottoman Empire up until the end of WWI and the British Empire for the next thirty years. Both of those empires used Jewish and Arab identities when it suited them, but Jewish Israelis weren't agents of either empire. No country sent Jewish colonists to the Holy Land to raid its resources and send back profits.

Despite Roman persecution and other obstacles, there has always been a Jewish minority in the land. That minority made an impact on the culture: Jewish tradition is full of rabbis, poets, and sages from different centuries who lived in what is now Israel. In general, modern Zionists came with a greater reverence for the land and its history than any empire brought to a colony. Far from exploiting the land, Zionists have worked to renew it. As just one example: the quarter of a billion trees planted in Israel over the last century have made it the only country on earth where there are *more* trees now than there were a hundred years ago.[11]

I think it's also important to look at where Zionists came from. They weren't like the English, French, or Spanish colonists sent around the world as their nations jockeyed for global power. We talk in the book about how Aaron's in-laws came from Iraq and an IDF soldier I met had roots in Yemen. It would be odd to cast Baghdadi or Yemeni Jews as imperial colonists a few borders away from their previous homes: I think people who call Israel a vestige of colonialism just ignore them. It's easier for people to paint Europeans as colonizers, but Europe isn't monolithic. Thinking about the specific places Zionists came from is a useful exercise.

Just look at our families. Romania, where your ancestors come from, and Ukraine, where mine come from, both spent

---

11. S. Ilan Troen, "Countering the BDS Colonial Settler Narrative," Academic Engagement Series Network Pamphlet Series no. 4 (April 2018).

time as parts of the Ottoman Empire, just like the Holy Land. Geographically, both are roughly as close to Israel as Yemen is! That distance, incidentally, is about the same as the distance between Oklahoma to California the Joads travel in *The Grapes of Wrath*. Many Jewish Zionists were closer to friends and relatives in the Holy Land than people might assume today.

It's common for there to be tensions between older residents and new arrivals in any place, but we make a mistake when we treat any one group as if they're not legitimate. Arabic-speaking Palestinians and Hebrew-speaking Jews both have various claims to connection to the land. So, for that matter, do guest workers from the Philippines. Some of those claims have to do with history and some have to do with their presence now. You wouldn't say that the Hopi have the only right to Arizona because they were there before the Navajo, Spanish-speaking settlers, Mormon pioneers, Chicago transplants like my mom, and brand-new immigrants from Asia. Instead, we believe in sorting out ways to live together.

It might be simpler to make a claim about whose land each square inch of the plant is, but that's not enough. A moral discourse about any conflict isn't just about figuring out which group is right. It's about figuring out how to balance competing legitimate claims in a way that preserves the greatest level of dignity to everyone involved.

Saying that Jews are colonizers and therefore don't belong is a cop out. It strikes me as a way to avoid hard questions about Jewish security and self-determination in the world's only country where the majority of the population is Jewish.

JG: What are your thoughts about recent wars between Israel and Hamas?

JO: My first thought is always to worry about people I know. During the 2021 conflict between Israel and Hamas, I wrote to distant cousins who live in Eilat and Ramat Aviv to see if they were safe. The Eilat branch of the family migrated from

Buenos Aires to Israel after a 1994 synagogue bombing became the worst terror attack in Argentine history. Eilat is a tourist destination on the Red Sea. My cousin Claudio didn't move there to antagonize anyone, but to build up a nice life and a career in the tourism industry. It's sad how attacks have followed his family even there.

I don't only worry about Jewish Israelis, though. Even if a conflict starts with Hamas outside Gaza, it can escalate quickly to affect Palestinians elsewhere. I also reached out to Besan Quffa to see how things were for her family in Ramallah. This past year, watching riots inside Israel, I worried about people in the Palestinian neighborhoods I visited as an intern promoting economic development.

I also wrote to members of the Tel Aviv Branch of the Church of Jesus Christ of Latter-day Saints who I knew and worshiped with—Filipinos, Russians, Ukrainians, Latinos, Armenians, Dutch, Americans, Israelis—all trying to live peaceful lives in greater Tel Aviv. They were on my mind because May 2021 was the first time Hamas rockets reached their area. No one in Israel is totally safe from these conflicts.

There are a lot of reasons why the situation got so out of control. I try to stay optimistic, but Hamas attacks have been really discouraging for me. For years, people talked about Israeli settlements within occupied Palestinian territories as one of the central obstacles to peace. The Israeli government ordered all Jewish settlers out of Gaza in 2005, but periodic attacks by Hamas on civilians have continued. For Israeli voters, that reality has reduced some of the commitment to negotiating peace. Instead, Israel and Egypt have focused on limiting the flow of goods into and out of Gaza. That makes life in Gaza harder to live, which fuels anger against Israel, which motivates more attacks. It's become a tragic cycle.

We need a way out. There are some signs, though, that people haven't given up. In June 2021, a coalition of parties created a new government. For the first time in Israel's history, an

Arab party joined the governing coalition as an official member. I don't know how things will develop going forward, but I celebrate steps forward.

JG: If you had it all to do again, do you think you'd choose the same life? Would you join the Church, make aliyah to Israel, come back to the United States for family and study and military service?

JO: I love God. I love my fellow men. By following the spiritual promptings I received, I've had wonderful opportunities to deepen my own discipleship and serve others. My life hasn't always been simple, but it's been good. Who could ask for anything more?

ACKNOWLEDGMENTS

◇

If it takes a village to raise a child, it took at least a small neighborhood of people to make this book. In addition to Sara Olson and Nicole Wilkes Goldberg, who helped us think through the ideas and keep our lives running while we spent weekends hunched over screens, we want to thank a long list of people who gave feedback on drafts, encouraged us, or helped pay for this project:

Lori Forsyth
Steve Evans
Michael Austin
Elder D. Todd
    Christofferson
Elder John Groberg
Judy Woolsey
Frank Clawson
Bradley Kramer
Shea Owens
David Thaxton
Lynda Thaxton
Matthew Nelson
Tracy Watson

Mark Diamond
Marci McPhee
David Benger
Tom Lewis
Rocky Nelson
Dr. Motti Inbari
Dr. Andrew Reed
Dr. Sara Hirschhorn
Dr. Miranda Wilcox
Dr. Morgan Davis
Dr. Shon Hopkin
Dr. Kimball Taylor
Dr. Ehud Eiran
Jenna Eve Ziegler

Rachel Alter
Joshua Borenstein
Kevin Blood
Sharon Bender
Brandt Peacock
Janci Patterson
Devin Toma
Jenna Carson
Noah Epstein
Terry Hardy Olsen
Tara Owens
Lynda Thaxton
Cassidy Owens Bastian
Yohei Araki

Corinda Kelly Krebs

Leanne Owens

Ken Reinstein

Missy Krohn

Dan Burner

Liz G Owens

Stephen K. Parkinson

Justin Chugg

Roscoe Scott Nelson

Steven Case

Sharon Bender

Zack Dees

Stephen Reimann

Stephanie Gabbitas

Kristine Balch Gerhart

Chris James

John Westhoff

Bryan Nelson

Yves Sighfreed

Yrma Salazar

Devin Toma

Grant Arnold

Christian David
Spendlove

Connor McBride

Bradford Family

Dave Cotts

Brandt Daniels

Nicki Williams

Thomas R Scott

Justin Ray

Christopher Bradford

Dan Ellsworth

Holly Schuetz

Lezlee Ellis Whiting

Linda J Cotton

April Henricks

Pj Harrigan

Rebecca Kojm

Saul Maldonado
Guardiola

Joah Fussell

Cris Baird

Merrijane Barton Rice

Gerry Hanni

Jim Kennard

Bryan Catanzaro

SPECIAL THANKS TO
JAMES GOLDBERG'S PATREON SUPPORTERS

We'd also like to express thanks to the people who provide regular support to James Goldberg's writing through his Patreon account. Figuring out how to tell our people's stories well takes time and resources. This book and many others are possible because of people who invest in the dream of a richer Mormon literature:

Bryan Catanzaro

Jared and Selina
Forsyth

Greta Hobbs

Andrea and Andrew
Hurst

David and Anne Healey

Devin and Marites
Galloway

Nick Senzee

Rosalie Stone

Cris and Janae Baird

David and Sunitha Gill

Jessica and Zac Wiest

Joah Fussell

Mark Olson

Anna Erickson

Annalisa Waite

Dan Call

Gene Jones

Heidi Creer

Hillary Stirling

James and Taylor Egan

Jason McDonald

Kate Shipman

Kayela Seegmiller

Kjerste Christensen

Merrijane Rice

Miranda Wilcox

Robert Bennett

Rosalynde Welch

Sheila Gill Hadden

Tony Gunn

Travis Austin

Adam and Laurie Stradling

Ardis E. Parshall

Ashley Gephart

Brian Ebie

Camilla Stark

Chris Burnham

Craig Yugawa

Elizabeth Mott

Ian McKnight

Jeanna Stay

Kami Bratten

The Kevin Klein family

Kristine Haglund

Melissa Leilani Larson

Peter Olson

Rebecca Bateman

Rebecca McCulloch

Ryan Saltzgiver

Scott and Pam Frost

Steve Otteson

Tanner Sperry

Vaughn Johnson

Walker Frahm

Andrea Landaker

Arlene Ball

Jennifer Eichelberger

Austin Smith

Benjamin Christensen

Christopher Bradford

Colleen Baker

Conrad Dietrick

Danielle Badger

Diantha Hopkins

Edward M. Goldberg

Eric D. Snider

The Jankovich Family

James Jones

Karl O.

Katherine Cowley

KyneWynn le Kind

Mattathias Westwood

Michael Haycock

Rachel Helps

Robison Wells

Jennifer and Ryan Rauzon

Stephen Whitaker

Tara Hawks

Taylor Petrey

Vilo Elisabeth Westwood

Vilo Westwood

Jason and Sarah Olson

William Morris

JASON OLSON is a graduate of Brigham Young University's Ancient Near Eastern Studies/Hebrew Bible program and received his Ph.D. from Brandeis University's Near Eastern and Judaic Studies program. He is the author of *America's Road to Jerusalem: The Impact of the Six-Day War on Protestant Politics* (Lexington Books, 2018), which further explores his ideas about Jewish-Christian relations, Zionism, and the US-Israel relationship. He proudly served as a U.S. Navy chaplain from 2014–2020, ministering to Sailors and Marines of all faiths.

JAMES GOLDBERG's family is Sikh on one side, Jewish on the other, and Mormon in the middle. He won the Association for Mormon Letters awards in Drama (2008, for *Prodigal Son*) and Novel (2012, for *The Five Books of Jesus*) and has been a finalist in Poetry, Creative Nonfiction, and Criticism. His recent collaborations include *The Bollywood Lovers' Club* (with Janci Patterson), *Song of Names: A Mormon Mosaic* (with Ardis Parshall) and the online multimedia project *A Dance of Light* (with Lisa DeLong and Nicole Pinnell).

Made in the USA
Las Vegas, NV
13 August 2024